# My Playboy Story

## Hopping from Richmond to Hollywood

**My Playboy Story: Hopping from Richmond to Hollywood**
Formerly "Everyone's Best Friend at Playboy"
Copyright ©2017 Malorie Mackey

ISBN 978-0-692-85111-1 PRINT
ISBN 978-0-692-85112-8 EBOOK


March 2017

Published and Distributed by
Malorie Mackey
www.MalorieMackey.com

Cover Design: Alex Hildebrand
Cover Photo Credit: Jay Ablah Photography
Cover Art: James McInerney
Cover Concept: Raquel Pomplun
Special Thanks: Dumont Marketing Group

   ISBN 978-0-692-85111-1, 978-0-692-85112-8 digital

1. BIOGRAPHY & AUTOBIOGRAPHY / General. 2. Entertainment & Performing Arts. 3. Rich & Famous.

# Acknowledgments

To everyone who helped sculpt my journey and to my friends and family.

To my supportive husband Damian who pushed me to make this book happen.

To my friend Jimmy who helped guide me through the entire process.

To my friends Raquel and Alex H. for their creativity.

To the Hefner family, especially to my good friend Marston, for allowing me into their world.

And to all the dreamers out there. May you tackle your dreams and live your lives to the fullest.

# My Playboy Story

## Hopping from Richmond to Hollywood

Malorie Mackey

# PREFACE

*From Pageantry to Playboy*

Let me begin this story by saying that I am the stereotypical "good girl." Many girls have looked at me and said, "You look extremely religious," or "You're so cute," and even, "I bet you never do anything wrong." My favorite question was, "Are you Amish?" Yes, someone really asked me that. And, for the record, no I am not Amish.

I grew up in a nice home in a beautiful woodland community in Virginia. I loved camping, being outdoors, and horseback riding. Nature is a very large part of who I am. My small group of friends and I would always find ourselves playing outdoors and enjoying the beautiful scenery that Virginia had to offer. Growing up, I excelled in both sports and academics, but, when I made my way into high school, I found my true passion in acting. I was drawn to the theatre like a moth to a flame, and I couldn't help but follow my desire.

As I studied theatre, there was a boy who stood by my side. His name was Damian. (I found out later that he joined theatre for me, and the theatre is exactly what brought us together.) We had gone to the same middle school, living near one another, and we had a friendship/romance that mirrored Winnie and Kevin from *The Wonder Years*. We grew together as artists, participating in five shows a year through our school. We graduated high school as a couple and wound up going to college together for performance. Dreaming was very important to us. What is life without dreams? We dreamed of moving to Los Angeles together and joining the industry, as we liked making films much more than we liked the stage. We would stay up late and talk on the phone or go out on long walks under the bright, shining stars and discuss the future that we would have together on the West Coast.

During my last year in college, I was offered a chance to model with Wilhelmina/Modelogic in Richmond, Virginia. I jumped on that opportunity and found myself print modeling. I had never thought that I was pretty enough to model before, but it was nice that the experience came around to prove me wrong. Though people would consistently tell me that I was pretty, I always saw myself as the girl next door, and I never saw the beauty that others did. It was because of my endeavors with Modelogic that I decided to pursue modeling alongside my acting career.

College graduation came around in the blink of an eye, and Damian and I knew what we wanted to do. We packed up our things and moved out to Los Angeles with a few friends. We drove across the country in a moving van and rented a small apartment in the valley. We were so happy to be living our dream together. We had grown up with each other, found love, and moved together as artists. I was still very naïve, but I had many dreams. I would never forget who I was or where I came from. My Virginia roots would shine through me forever, no matter what. I was very set on that. I wasn't going to let myself be changed by whatever Los Angeles threw my way. I didn't know what to expect in LA, but I was ready for it.

That being said, I was as surprised as anyone to find myself in the world of Playboy. I am quite the prude. I tend to hide the fact that I even remotely have breasts under large sweaters or slightly baggy t-shirts, I like to go barefoot, and I can definitely be a tomboy. I am put off by overly sexual women and am embarrassed to talk about sex. In fact, my story in Los Angeles started in the world of pageantry.

In theory, pageantry seemed to fit my personality better, but, in reality, that just wasn't the case. I found myself competing as Miss Ventura Blvd in Miss California USA during November of 2010, just shortly after our move.

On the outside, it seems like a wonderful opportunity with the nicest girls, which was why I jumped on the chance to compete, but the rules and regulations were enough to drive anyone mad. We were not allowed out of our rooms after a certain time, otherwise we would be disqualified, and we could not be found wandering at any time without our roommates. Despite the dreadful book of rules, the pageant threw its own rulebook out the window nightly, keeping us out later than our curfew. They would keep us out rehearsing until 1am, and then we would be required to be up and makeup ready at 6am, so we would really only get 3-4 hours of sleep a night. I couldn't handle that stress on my body. I needed sleep. By the end of the weekend, all of the girls were falling asleep backstage at the event.

I did not win, but, somehow, I received the Friend's Choice Award, which was their equivalent of the "People's Choice" based on an online voting system. It was a great honor. That being said, I was shocked to win anything because the world of pageantry wasn't my cup of tea. I was persuaded into it by a promoter on one of my first auditions. I was a sweet, soft girl from Virginia, and these pageant girls were out for blood. I seemed to fit in very well, but I lacked the claws, nails, and back-stabbing abilities that these pageant girls had. (Don't get me wrong, some of them were very sweet, but the real competitors weren't like that.)

So how did I make the leap from pageantry to pinup? Well, I wasn't entirely turned off from the world of pageantry after the Miss California USA event (surprisingly enough), but Playboy was always more appealing to me. I used to laugh at the pageant girls back at home because I was much more into sports than beauty. I would find myself watching *The Girls Next Door*, and I longed to be at the Playboy Mansion. Visiting the Playboy Mansion became a dream of mine. The type of beauty that Playboy promoted was what I wanted to have. I wanted to be at the Playboy Mansion having fun like all the girls on TV. So, when I was offered the chance to jump past pageantry to the world of Playboy, I did it in a heartbeat.

This is a true story. Every situation is factual and adapted from journal entries I wrote after the events. Everyone I mention is a real person; however, I am changing some of their names to keep their privacy. My journey begins after I decided to move to Los Angeles to pursue my acting and modeling career. I only knew what life was like in Virginia, and LA was very different from that.

MALORIE MACKEY

# PART 1
## My Journey to the Playboy Mansion

# Meeting Russell

Late one night, I was reviewing casting submissions on a site where companies put up job listings for models. Damian and I had finally gotten settled in from our big move across the country. It took us a couple of months to get our lives in order and our apartment set up the way we wanted it to be, but it was worth the wait. My father had brought my cat out across the country for me a month after our move, and I was happy that our family was together again. We were finally set up in Los Angeles. I was basking in the "completeness" that I felt now that everything at our new home was the way I wanted it to be. I was on course to accomplish all of my dreams, and I wasn't going to take no for an answer.

I was set on getting myself off of the ground as quickly as possible. I would sit around, daily, and submit myself to castings on multiple networks. Though we didn't have any money to our name, I would scrounge around enough to be listed on all the major casting sites. I was focused on my dream of being a working actress and model, and I was going to do everything I could to get there. I was excited to get my career rolling, as I knew that once it gained momentum, it would start snowballing into something great.

On this particular evening, I had just come off of working long hours at my day job. (When I first moved from Virginia, I worked at Victoria's Secret for a year or so to afford to live.) Though I felt the exhaustion weighing down my body like sandbags, I managed to keep going. I sat down at my computer to review all of the castings that I wasn't around to submit for during the day. Better late than never, right?

My eyes were tired, but I was on a mission to find work. Through this particular site, I met one of the casting directors for Playboy. We'll call him Russell. Russell was "the big deal" in the LA nightlife (or so he thought) because he casted models for the Playboy Mansion events. He found pretty girls and offered them free entrance into certain Playboy

Mansion parties. Not to mention, he casted for *Playboy* TV and a lot of *Playboy Special Edition* magazines. I wasn't interested in being nude, but I was definitely a fan of *The Girls Next Door*, and, as I mentioned before, it was a dream of mine to make it to the Mansion at least once. Luckily, Damian supported me chasing after my dreams and was okay with me trying to go to the Playboy Mansion.

On this particular night, through a listing, I saw that Russell was looking for girls to go with him to a Playboy Mansion event. It was the annual Halloween party. Halloween was my favorite holiday, so I had to chance contacting him. I eagerly messaged him about the event. To my surprise, he quickly responded back and invited me to meet him for a casting at a popular club in Hollywood later that week. He said to go there, mention his name, and they would let me in immediately. Now, looking back, it was too presumptuous of me to meet someone for a casting at a night club. That is something I would never do now. That isn't the type of work I would want. Perhaps it was because of Russell that I learned this lesson?

The night of the casting came, and I was, surprisingly, more nervous than normal. I loved what I did, but auditioning was always something that made me nervous. Though I had confidence in my work, knowing that I was being judged and evaluated during castings always gave me a little anxiety before meeting the casting directors.

After spending thirty minutes looking for parking, I arrived at the club. (It really shouldn't have taken that long to find parking in Los Angeles, but I never had to worry about parking in Virginia. Where I came from, everything was mostly suburban, and, even in the valley, parking was easy to come by. I was not used to the city.) When I finally found parking, I had to tip-toe around in heels from the lot to the front of the club. I approached the bouncers, and they let me in with no questions asked in front of everyone. I was sent right to Russell's table. At the time, this was his signature club and his signature table. It was the first table on the left as you made your way into the commotion. As

I walked over to it, I couldn't help but feel nervous. I had spent hours preparing my hair and makeup to make myself look like what I thought was the spitting image of a Playboy Bunny. This was my first time at any club ever, and I was wearing skinny jeans and a pink leopard top. I should have been embarrassed. My outfit gave away that I had never been to a club before, and I'm pretty sure that Russell wanted to puke when he saw me. You could tell that I was completely out of my element.

I arrived, shyly, to the table to find that it was empty. The security guard standing by the table told me that Russell was on his way, so I should sit back and be patient. Fortunately for me, I only had to wait about ten minutes. When I least expected it, in walked a hipster-looking man with a posse of twelve nearly-identical girls and an extremely hot female assistant who happened to be wearing lingerie. In fact, all these girls were wearing next to nothing. The assistant had a French maid outfit on that barely covered her private areas. This was the little girl from Virginia's first brush with Playboy (or what I thought was Playboy), and I didn't know how to react. Russell greeted me, shook my hand, and gave me a card. His "assistant" (we'll call her Vanessa) took my picture and saved it on her phone. Her bleach blonde hair was as vibrant as the flash on her phone. (They were very fake, but they were nice to me.) At the time, I thought they were generally sincere, but knowing who Russell is and what I was wearing, I'm sure he didn't want me around. He told me to relax and have fun with everyone. All the drinks were on him.

I sat down at the circular table and awkwardly looked around. I tried to say something to the girl next to me, but she wasn't paying attention. Because I didn't feel comfortable in the club, I was coming off more awkward than normal. Finally, one of the girls started a conversation with me. She asked me where I was from (it was obvious by my virgin hair and out-of-style fashion that I wasn't from LA), and the conversation took off from there.

After jabbering with these girls, I found that they had piled out from a limo. They rode with Russell to the club to make him look good. He had the best table, the best service, and the "best" girls with him to make himself look better than anyone there. Reflecting now, I realize that they were all desperate "wannabes" who had no idea what Playboy was really like. Russell's girls are the girls that give Playboy a bad name.

I didn't know exactly what to do. I didn't drink, but they sure did. In fact, they were all drinking a lot, which meant that they were opening up a lot. They all spilled the same story about being a model just dying to get famous. Most had been in *Playboy Special Editions* already. They came from all over the country, some from all over the world, to "live it up." Now, I am not one for parties. I have never been drunk because I have always been afraid of losing control. This experience was a shock for me. I was not a club person or a party person, and the flashing lights and mind-shattering music was too much for me to deal with. It was nice to talk to some of the girls, although, when I turned down the free drinks, they looked at me like I was crazy!

Then, the shock of the night came! There was a personal bouncer at Russell's table. He stopped all of the girls who tried to jump up and join Russell's group. I saw a few girls approach, and the bouncer would stop them, get Russell's attention, and turn their heads with his hand to "present" the girls to him for approval. If he approved, they could come up. If not, they had to go away. Russell would only let the "prettiest girls" up at his table. (But, let's be honest, the "prettiest" girls, in his opinion, were the ones with the fakest appearance. The girls with the largest implants and firmest faces always won his heart.) I began to question why I was there. That wasn't me in the least.

I couldn't believe my eyes. I'd never seen anything like it. A guy piles girls out of a limo, squeezes them all into a small table, and then uses a bouncer to humiliate girls that he doesn't think are hot enough! That was too much for me. I guess it was a good sign that I was up there, though.

I had an event that following morning, so I ran home after only an hour or so. It was an experience I was not soon to forget. I was innocent and young, and that was my first taste of the crazy LA nightlife.

After the event, I had to check in and make sure that I could go to the Mansion with Russell. I waited and waited for what seemed liked years. Realistically, after a week of waiting, I emailed Russell to check in. I asked if there was anything he needed me to do, and I thanked him for meeting with me. I didn't hear from him for a very long time. (In fact, my Miss California USA pageant happened over this period of silence from Russell, thus ending my life in the pageant world completely.)

He replied a month or so later. I had to set up a profile on a website to be accepted to the Mansion parties. They would send me a "golden ticket" once I was approved and used his code. Well, he told me too late, and I couldn't get into the Halloween party. That was unfortunate. Perhaps Russell didn't have the power or control that I thought he did?

From that moment on, I received casting notices from Russell on a bi-monthly basis. They were mass emails that went out to everyone. I attempted to come in for non-nude and party castings on more than one occasion, but none of them were successful. After a month or so of not seeing Russell and his crew, I knew that I was going to have to commit if I wanted to reach my goal and go to the Playboy Mansion. I saw a casting to attend a new night club with Russell in my inbox one day. I decided to email him to see if I could be a part of the event. He responded and gave me his number. I texted him and, somehow, got in the group. It happened to be sheer luck, I guess. He gave me his address and told me to meet him there. We'd go from there to the new club. He said to bring a friend, so I brought my friend Kara. I was concerned about going out with Russell again, but with a friend I felt more secure.

# The Hierarchy

Kara and I arrived at Russell's house for the first time on a very cold night in November. He lived in a nice-sized mansion located in Encino, and I expected to see the infamous limo and, at least, twelve girls waiting for us like before. To my surprise, there was no limo. Even more surprising, there were only three other girls. We rang the doorbell and stepped back onto the marble staircase to get a better view of the stone structure of the entrance. As I shivered a bit in the cold, I could vaguely hear the pitter patter of heels clumping on a hard wood floor from behind the door. They were getting closer and closer until Vanessa, the sexy assistant, answered the door and let us in. Fortunately, this time she had more clothes on. She was wearing a tight-fitted, mini strapless dress rather than lingerie. It squeezed her form so tightly that I had to wonder how she managed to put it on in the first place. Despite having the appearance of a bombshell, she was actually quite soft-spoken. She quietly said "Hi" and led us upstairs to the other girls. With this, my life was inadvertently changed. I was slowly heading to where I needed to be at this time in my life, but I wasn't too happy about it. You see, I was a homebody. My favorite activities were painting or watching movies at home with Damian. Going out was definitely not something I enjoyed, but I was on a mission.

The three girls that accompanied Kara and I that evening became pivotal characters in this part of my story. Let me introduce you to them in more depth. Vanessa, the assistant, was actually Russell's girlfriend. She was the "queen bee." Watching Vanessa was like watching the movie *Mean Girls* unfold in real life. She was pretty, in a Barbie-like way. As I mentioned before, her hair was bleached blonde and she wore a lot of makeup. Dark eyeliner and fake eyelashes were a must for her. (She joked with me later that Russell wouldn't let her go out unless she had eyeliner in the inner ring around her eye. It makes them look darker and adds the illusion of more makeup.) Her daily wardrobe consisted of expensive heels and short, short dresses that made sure her breasts were featured. Most of the time she wore lingerie sets and slips as if they were dresses. She was very sweet, but she was guarded, and, the more you got to know her, the more you understood why she was like that. Generally, if you spent time together, she'd throw one or two "Are you having fun?" type questions at you. For those of you that love the movie *Mean Girls*, she was the Regina George character in my life.

Next, Kristina was the "second-in-command," so to speak. She was Vanessa's best friend. (I'm also pretty sure that Russell was in love with her, but that's just a theory.) She was cute, youthful (only 19), and sweet (until she got drunk—then she would attack everyone that she secretly didn't like). She took a liking to me. She was the Gretchen Wieners of this part of my life. Regardless, we got along really well for a time. She was the easiest person for me to relate to because she was young, as I was, and she was a small-town girl from Connecticut, so we both came from the East Coast. However, she let LA get to her and control her. She was not afraid to run wild. I was never wild—not for a second. I would just go along with her shenanigans. She was the first in the loose chain of people to refer to me as a "best friend."

Finally, there's Melina. Melina was the girl who was always there but never got any attention. She tried out for Playboy and never got cast for anything. She had been hanging around with Russell for years and had nothing to show for it except the few scars she got from falling all over herself while she was drunk. She was also known for being a whore. Yes, she was the whore of the group (the Karen), and everyone knew it. I found out later that she actually *was* a whore! She had a couple of sugar daddies who paid her for sex, and there was a younger, married man who did the same. Sleeping with men was all she did to make money. She would talk about her sexual endeavors as easily as she would talk about her day to day life, and I would just giggle and try to hide my face when she did, because no one was surprised by any of her stories. She did anything and everything. Talking about sex made me very uncomfortable, so she took some getting used to on my part. She desensitized me to that subject a bit.

These three girls decorated my life over the next year as I went on my endeavors with Russell. They were masters of the club scene, trotting around in next to nothing like they owned the night, and I was the little shadow hiding behind them. They introduced me to their crazy world, and I stayed out of the limelight as much as possible as I followed their story.

# Bar 210

After arriving at Russell's during the evening in question, we stood around, waited for Russell to get ready, and then headed out to the club. The four of us who weren't Russell and Vanessa squeezed into the back of Russell's car. They started playing mind-shattering music in his shiny, brand-new Mercedes, and everyone sang along until we got to our destination. Looking at Russell and Vanessa from the back seat, I saw just how much they thought they were a Hollywood power couple. She was a bleached-blonde Barbie who lived to party and cling to his success, and he was "the man" with the nice car and giant ego.

We arrived at the club and were escorted out of the car. Russell would never do anything to hurt his image, so, naturally, he paid a valet to take the car so we could head right in to his private table where several of his friends had already gathered. The table at this particular lounge had a really nice set up. It was a black metallic table with a dark velvet sofa behind it. Above the back of the sofa was a hanging waterfall of tiny metallic beads that fell down from the ceiling. You could stand on a small ledge behind the sofa next to the wall and hold onto the beads for stability.

We sat on the top part of the sofa, and the waitress didn't hesitate to pour our drinks. Then, just like that, I actually bonded with the three regular girls that were there, which carved my destiny to keep coming back. The bonding happened because Jennifer showed up. I owe it all to her. Jennifer did not possess the stereotypical image of beauty. She had some extra weight on her, and her bitter attitude gave her a sour appeal. As soon as she showed her face, Kristina's eyes narrowed. Kristina turned to me and started ranting about how evil this girl was. Apparently, Jennifer was telling everyone that she was "one of Russell's girlfriends." Kristina assured me that "Russell is not Hugh Hefner. He has one girlfriend, and he loves her very much!" (That actually reassured me at the time, because I wasn't sure. The way he was, they could all have been his girlfriends, and I was not about to be on his menu.)

My friend Kara started egging Kristina on more and more. She would listen and then chime in, "That BITCH!" The drunker Kristina got, the more things she hated about Jennifer, and she loved to tell me about it in extreme detail. Sadly, that is how we bonded. Finally, Kristina marched over to Jennifer. She was drunk, so she thought she was whispering to her, but, the fact was, the entire table could hear the loud murmurings of her voice. She stayed there for a long time, and we all watched, wondering what was really happening. After a few minutes, Kristina came back. She was looking very full of herself. A few minutes later, Vanessa got a text from Jennifer that said, "Sorry I came." The lesson that I learned that night: Kristina hates everyone who isn't Vanessa (and later me) when she's drunk... and, sometimes, she fought us, too. I turned away from Kristina after she sat back down and focused on my drink.

Let me take a moment to explain to you how I "drink" at these events. It's a tradition that I started that night and have held onto to the present day. To me, this type of clubbing event was a job. I was doing it to further myself and to get in good with the people I should know—at the time, that was Russell. I felt that I needed to be of right mind at these events, unlike the other girls who got plastered, so, I made sure that I poured my own drinks every time. If there was orange juice around, I put it in a cup with ice and pretended that there was liquor in it. I did the same with red bull or anything that could look like a drink. I never drank at these events, at all. I don't like drinking alcohol, and I couldn't trust the people I was with, so why would I?

On that night, I found out how right I was to not trust Russell. I saw Russell pull a vial out of his pocket while he was sitting next to me. He pulled out a key, put it in the vial, and the key came out with white powder on it. It took a minute for it to sink in, but I realized that Russell and his guy friends were putting cocaine on a key and then snorting it... in public. I had never seen anyone do drugs before and it frightened me a little. I was just praying he wouldn't offer it to me. The heavens answered my prayers, and he put it away after only a few minutes. I still couldn't fathom who would be stupid enough to do that in a public place.

When the clock struck 2am, the club closed, and we were ushered out of the building in herds. (You see, Russell always stayed until the party was over or the club was closing.) Jennifer was waiting outside in her car. Apparently she never left but had been waiting for Russell outside. She called to Russell and announced that she was coming to his place for the "after party." Furious, Kristina walked over to her and screamed into her car window, "The event is cancelled. Go home!"

Jennifer looked pathetically sad, "But I want some crack from him."

"He doesn't have any. Go home!" Kristina then stormed past us and jumped in Russell's Mercedes. We rode home, and all was eerily quiet. I, however, knew not to trust anyone enough to go inside to the "after party," so my friend and I split when we got back to where my car was waiting for me at Russell's place. And that, my friends, was my first true night out with Russell. I'm sure you can already tell several reasons why I grew to despise this man very quickly.

After that night at Bar 210, I tried my best to go out with Russell's posse at least once a week. Generally, this happened on Saturday nights, and Bar 210 was the place to be for a while. I was taken in by the three main girls immediately. They called me their "baby." They constantly babbled on about giving me sexy dresses, make-overs, tans, and more. They wanted to turn me into their project. My life was reenacting the events of *Mean Girls*, and I was the Lindsay Lohan character getting molded like plastic. Except, I didn't really fall for any of it. In *Mean Girls*, Cady gets wrapped up in everything. I was more aware of my surroundings than that. I was watching the crazy events happen around me rather than participating in them. I had promised myself that I wasn't going to change, and I was going to hold onto that promise. I may have gotten my hair highlighted, but changing my hair did not mean changing my personality.

I always met the group at Russell's house, but some of the other girls met us at the club. At times, it would just be four or five girls, and we would go out in Russell's car. Then, there were outings that Russell dubbed "Special Events." On these occasions, there were anywhere from 15 to 35 girls, and we would go in a limo, whether it be his normal limo or his huge hummer limo, to the club. It was on these nights that we had to make sure to dress nicer than normal or Russell would call us out for not looking our best. We could only go to the bathroom in small groups approved by him so he always had a lot of girls around him. To be honest, it was quite sickening. The more I was around his lifestyle, the more I wanted out. I would get frustrated and, instinctually, try to fight him, but I would stop myself before I started attacking him for the way he acted. The other girls seemed to act like this was normal behavior, but I had never seen a man treat women like they were his property before. This was new to me, and I really hated it.

One weekend, when we went back out to Bar 210, the owner of the club, who Kristina dubbed "Creepy Owner," started falling for her. He would pull her aside, treat her special, and take her to the bathroom next door in his private penthouse so she didn't have to wait in the long lines inside the club. Finally, he pulled her aside and said, "Hey. This doesn't have to be weird. You don't need to be uncomfortable because of my wife and kids. We can still make this work."

Kristina's jaw dropped. She was incredibly confused because nothing was going on between them. She knew now, though, that in his mind there was something there. She decided that it was best to play nice and be really sweet to him without leading him on. It didn't really work. Everywhere she was in the club, there was Creepy Owner. He was always right behind her no matter what. She would pull on my arm and go, "Oh my God. Do you see this? He's just standing right there staring at me!" And he always was.

The following week, we celebrated Kristina's official release into the *Playboy* magazine circuit. She was a cover model for a *Playboy Special Edition* magazine. We all got together, took pictures, and rode in the hummer limo to the club. For this event, there were at least 20 girls, so Russell was feeling particularly full of himself. Creepy Owner was so excited for Kristina. Based on the release and his newfound love for her, he bought a tower of cheesecake-filled pops that came in with a big sparkler on top. It was very nice. She, however, was still creeped out by him. No kind gesture that the owner could do would be of any use now that she knew what his intentions were.

It was on this night that I started to realize something odd and a little unsettling. Let me start by saying that I was grateful because Vanessa and Russell knew and respected the fact that I was in a relationship. Throughout my endeavors with them, I was with Damian, and they never forced me into anything or asked me to do anything sexual. That being said, I began noticing that Russell would grab a lot of these girls' butts. He'd grope them in passing and pull up their dresses to see the underwear they were wearing. After talking with a lot of the regular girls, I found out that Russell and Vanessa had more or less slept with everybody but me, Kristina, and a girl named Destiny (who we'll talk about later). They would have countless threesomes and foursomes with whoever Russell wanted... whenever he wanted. Most of the time with his girlfriend, of course. I came to notice that the ones who held out and didn't have sex with them got the farthest and stayed around the longest.

(Granted, they never asked me or Destiny because they knew that we were in relationships, which I appreciated.) It was disgusting. Russell was using the fact that he casted for *Playboy TV* as a catalyst to sleep with a lot of clueless wannabes who never had a chance in *Playboy*. He would convince them that they'd have a chance if they slept with him and Vanessa. Even worse, he would tell them he could make them Playmates, which he definitely had no ability to do.

One of the nights, when we were being ushered out of this new club at closing time, I caught part of a conversation that I shouldn't have heard. Vanessa leaned over to Kristina and whispered (loudly, because she was drunk), "Russell wants to have a THREESOME with us tonight!" She partially giggled at the word "threesome." Vanessa looked so excited and so proud of herself. She turned to her best friend to see her reaction.

Kristina was not amused, "What the hell!? Seriously!?"

"Yeah! Isn't that great!"

"That's disgusting! No offense, but I would never sleep with you. Or him. Either one of you. That's gross."

"What?" At this point, Vanessa looked like someone had just punched her in the gut.

Kristina just glared at her, "We're like family! You are basically my sister. You shouldn't let him do that to you. You know what? I can't keep quiet anymore. A relationship is between TWO PEOPLE! TWO PEOPLE! Are you too drunk to understand that?"

As we walked to the car, Melina and I stayed awkwardly silent as we heard Kristina repeat over and over again that a relationship was between two people. As the valet pulled their car around, Vanessa had enough. She started crying and ran to the passenger seat of the car. Kristina was still ranting about it even in Vanessa's absence. She coldly turned to Russell and said, "You better go see your girlfriend. You've pissed her off."

Russell looked amused, "Now what?"

"I don't know. Go fix it."

Kristina turned to Melina, "Am I wrong? I feel that someone should say these things to her. I don't get why she lets him do that. She hates doing it! She told me he makes her. Am I wrong?"

"You're not wrong. I just don't have the balls to say it like you do," croaked Melina. (It's funny that she said this, by the way, because Melina had slept with them a lot.)

That night ended with everyone making up, but that was the first peepshow I got from the crazy sexual endeavors of Vanessa and Russell. And, let me tell you, it only got worse as time went on.

# The Bikini Bar

Time passed and I became a regular member of Russell's crew. I didn't enjoy myself, but I began getting stuck in the routine of going out with them. Plus, I still felt that, maybe, Russell could help me with my career.

I would come home and vent to Damian about how horrible Russell and Vanessa were. He was worried for me, but he also trusted my judgement. He knew that I would make good decisions. At home, we were very happy. Damian was working as a waiter, and I was working at Victoria's Secret, still. Despite work, we had a lot of time at home to submit ourselves, go on auditions, and have our hobbies. I had already gotten a print and commercial agent, and I was auditioning regularly. I was happy with where I was, and I was still hoping that Russell might be able to take me further with my career. I wasn't sure how, but I had that strange feeling that he could help.

The more I went out with them, the closer Kristina and I became. I watched as Kristina started to develop feelings for Nick Hogan, son of Pro Wrestler Hulk Hogan. After meeting him once, Kristina was smitten. There was a random week night where Russell requested that we all go out to a bikini bar with him. Nick happened to join us. Kristina was so excited to see him again. The second she heard that he was coming, she decided that she loved him, and that he would be hers. Her mind was set. She did not know him well enough to justify texting him, so she got Russell to text him every five minutes to ensure that he was actually coming. When he came in, I thought she was going to pass out. He came over, said "Hi," stayed for about five minutes, then went to get food. During his food run, she made Russell text him every minute to see if he liked her or thought that she was hot.

Kristina was getting anxious, "You're not saying it right. You have to text him that—never mind. Give me your phone. I'll do it myself!"

Russell just laughed as she snatched the phone from his hand to type the messages herself. And then everything got silent for three seconds before Kristina exploded, "WHAT!!?? I'm an 8.5!?"

Russell was silent.

"I hate you. How could you!? I can't believe it! This isn't right at all. How could you?"

Russell got defensive, "This is from way back. Before I knew you!"

Vanessa decided to add to the conversation, "You know, I was less than that. He only changed my number after I found out what he put me in as and cried. Then he made me 'Super Model 11'."

I was very confused as to what just happened, "What's going on?"

Vanessa turned to me "Russell rates the girls he saves in his phone on a hotness scale from 1 to 10. It helps for when he casts."

I looked dumbfounded, "Ooooooh..."

Kristina, who was oblivious to the fact that Vanessa and I were talking at all, jumped right back in, "Why am I an 8? WHY AM I AN 8!?"

"Because you wouldn't take your pants off. I had to deduct 1.5 points," Russell said very casually.

This had to be clarified for me, which it immediately was. When Kristina came in to audition for *Playboy TV* (about a year prior to this), she didn't know Vanessa or Russell. That was how they met and, in turn, became best friends. Well, she was so nervous when she had to take off her clothes at the casting that she didn't take her pants off at all and took pictures and video with her pants on. Somehow, she still got cast, and they have not let her forget this since. For the rest of the night I heard Kristina yell about how she was only an 8, and she never stopped.

That same night, we went out to eat after the bar. I neglected to bring up that the event at the bikini bar was a lingerie party, so everyone was in some type of sleepwear. Everyone was in conservative lingerie, except Melina. Again, this was no shock to anyone because she was the promiscuous one. She wore a thong, a bra, a pair of high heels, and nothing else. When we went to eat, we all covered up with jackets so we didn't look like, well, whores. Melina didn't care. She showed up in her short leather jacket and a thong. She paraded into the restaurant like that. Everyone stared at her. They were all horrified. We sat down, enjoyed a nice meal with meaningless conversation, laughed at the fact that Melina was just in lingerie, and then piled out. As we left, an elderly waitress held the door open for us, as if she couldn't be happier that we were leaving. She had the most wide-eyed look when Melina passed by, and that was the funniest thing I had seen in a while. I completely understood. I empathized with everyone staring at us. Who would ever go out in a thong without pants on? This was something that, even in LA, isn't very common to see. It was funny, but also a little disturbing.

# Being in Russell's Elite

Time moved along, and, with it, Russell jumped from club to club as if they were all passing fads. We bounced from bikini bar to dance club to whatever else was cool at the time. I pretended to be enjoying myself, even though I actually dreaded going out. Don't get me wrong, I had fun with Kristina, but the club life was not for me. At this point in my life, Damian and I had started planning our wedding. We had been together for so many years that we figured it was time to tie the knot. We were excited, but we always knew that it would happen. I craved to be at home watching movies with him. Home life was what I really wanted. Along with that, Damian and I had started working on a small string of Indie films. When we were filming, we worked 6 days out of the week and got very little rest. Luckily for me, I could take off the time at Victoria's Secret to make these movies happen when they would come up. On top of that, I worked hard during the day auditioning and filming, and I just wanted to go home and relax. I hated the nightlife, and I thought that both Russell and Vanessa were horrible people. But, I had a goal, and I wasn't about to let it go. I was sure that if I got to know Russell well enough, he just had to take me to the Playboy Mansion with him at some point. The way things were going, there was no way he could not! I was part of the in-crowd, and I was getting restless. When were my constant efforts going to pay off? I was, seemingly, a best friend to the group, and I was truly a best friend to Kristina... something good had to come from this horror, right?

There was one night that always stood out in my mind where we were celebrating Kristina's release into another *Playboy* magazine, and she was not happy about it. I went out with her earlier that day, and we went shopping for the perfect outfit. (Russell told her that she had to be the best-dressed girl there because it was her party.) As we shopped around for her dress, she flooded me with a river of secrets. She told me that she secretly hated Russell. He was always telling her how to dress and how to act. She said that she hated the way he told her when she could and couldn't use the bathroom. She also poured out how much she hated the way he treated Vanessa. She said that sometimes she felt bad for her because she let these things happen to herself, but she was tired of listening to Vanessa cry about being forced into countless threesomes with aspiring Playboy models. I responded to her by telling her how much the club life really wasn't for me. Apparently Kristina felt just as out of place as I did with the group. That was refreshing for me to hear. No wonder I liked her so much. We were a lot more alike than I thought.

After four hours of looking, we were unable to find a dress that Kristina liked, so she picked out a corset top, and we went to Russell's to get ready for Kristina's party in his spare room. When the time came for the party, she was frustrated that there were close to 20 girls that she didn't know coming over for the event. She hated that, because most of them knew who she was, and she didn't care who they were. All of Russell's girls that went out with him once or twice looked up to Kristina because she had tested for Playmate, and you could tell that, next to his girlfriend, Kristina was Russell's favorite.

I think that Russell loved Kristina. I think that he'd never end his relationship with Vanessa because it was too easy, and it'd be too inconvenient for him to do so because she lived with him and worked as his assistant. But he did want Kristina. For instance, he forgot his anniversary with Vanessa, and he forgot her birthday, but when a song played in the car on the way to a club one night, he said, "This is your song, Kristina!"

"Why is it my song?" Kristina blinked.

"When you first hung out with us, this song played, and you bounced around to it like crazy. It reminds me of you." When a guy remembers another girl bouncing around to some random song, but doesn't remember his own anniversary or his girlfriend's birthday, that's suspicious.

Right before Kristina's party began, she tried on her new corset top and went into Russell and Vanessa's room to present it to them. Russell responded with, "What the hell are you wearing? You can't wear that. You have to wear a dress. The girls are going to be looking to you to be impressive because tonight's party is for you. Go change."

Kristina glared at him, "I couldn't find a dress."

"Wear one of Vanessa's."

"Seriously?"

"Yes. This isn't a game."

Kristina was pissed. She stormed back to the spare room almost in tears. Holding back her rage, she regurgitated what we had been talking about earlier. "They tell me how to dress and act. They tell me to represent them at all times and be beautiful. I can't wear jeans or sweats, and my hair and makeup always have to be a certain way. I hate it!"

They had started to push this stuff on me, but I, mostly, ignored it and played dumb. They weren't at the point of drilling it into me as they were doing to poor Kristina, and, at this point, she was fed up. She was tired of Russell and Vanessa. She was going to be leaving for Connecticut the following week to visit her family for a month, and she just started a relationship with Nick Hogan. She wanted to see him before she left, and that didn't look likely with the circumstances of the evening. Kristina decided that she was going to go out and see Nick, somehow.

Not five minutes after we arrived at the club, Kristina came over to me and said, "On the count of three, you're going to go outside and meet me. Just run!"

I was clueless, "What?"

"One, two, three-go!" She grabbed my arm and heaved forward, jerking me out of the seat I was in. She dragged me passed the table and towards the front of the club. I stopped for a second, looking oddly confused, and she just carelessly smiled and explained, "I knew that they wouldn't let me leave my own party, but if they're drunk enough, they probably won't even notice that we're gone."

Suddenly, Nick Hogan pulled up with some dirty-looking, ill-mannered guy and his girl. They told us to hop in, and he drove over to another brand new club. It was a crazy, interesting, wild club with three rooms and walls made of tin, aluminum, and velvet. The bouncer looked the other way because Nick was a celebrity, and he allowed us into the bar—no questions asked, no IDs checked. We were led into the back of the club by our own personal body guard. He stood at the table with us the whole night. With him, another bouncer kept coming over to present girls to Nick that he thought he'd like. That was incredibly awkward, seeing as Kristina was with him. I was definitely nervous about being out with Kristina and Nick, seeing as I didn't know Nick well. I stood around pretending not to be bored while Kristina made out with Nick all night.

Luckily, he wound up being very sweet. He didn't drink all night, and he took us right back to Russell's when the club closed.

We arrived back at Russell's place just as the limo was pulling up to release Russell and his girls. They all went in, and I followed the back of the herd so I could go up to the guest room and get my belongings that had been left up there from earlier that day. Then, as I walked through the door, I heard Russell and Vanessa announce from the top of the stairs, "We're going up to our room. No one bother us for a while!" They dragged two girls up with them and slammed the door. It didn't take an imagination to figure out what they were doing. I just ignored it and went into the guest room to get my stuff. Kristina followed me in and came up to get her stuff, as well. She missed Russell's announcement because she was saying goodbye to Nick. One of Vanessa's dresses was on the bed because Kristina had tried it on earlier, so, naturally, she decided to return it to her. She went to their bedroom door and tried to open it. It was locked. She wasn't impressed, so she knocked.

"Kristina. Don't go in there. They went in there with two other girls." I whispered from down the hall.

"Oh My God! They're having sex!?" She began banging on the door over and over again.

I didn't want either one of us to get involved, so I called to Kristina again, "Don't bother them!"

"Vanessa, you can't cry to me about this anymore. If you have sex with different girls every weekend, you let it happen. You're letting this happen, and I won't let you bitch to me about it!" She screamed through the door.

Vanessa opened the door in her pajamas. The other two girls left the room giggling, and Russell was in his bed under the covers with no shirt on and his hands up... as if he was very satisfied.

Vanessa looked at Kristina, "What's wrong?"

"I can't believe you! You bitch to me every day about how Russell makes you have sex with a different girl or two every weekend, but you still do it. You just did it again and you could have said, 'No.' You didn't stop it. I have nothing to say to you, and I don't want to hear you complain about it ever again. You have the ability to stop it!" With that, Kristina stormed down the stairs and out the door. Vanessa tried to follow her, but she was so drunk that she couldn't catch her. (I'd like to point out that Vanessa and Kristina were best friends, but, at this point in their friendship, they fought almost every time they were drunk. And, like clockwork, they always made up by the next day. It was an endless cycle, and this particular fight was no exception to that.)

The following night, they got into an even funnier fight. We were leaving the club, and this time, we had come in Russell's car. There were six of us all together, and as we approached his Mercedes, Kristina began shouting that she had watched each person drink. She announced that we all must be drunk. She said that she wouldn't get in the car because she didn't want to die. (This happened every time she got extremely intoxicated, which was often.) She just stood outside the car with her arms crossed in frustration. I tried to be the solution because, generally, she let me drive because she knew that I didn't drink, but she was too angry to listen to anyone. A brunette model from *Playboy TV* who happened to be with us said, "I'll do it."

Kristina yelled at her, "I don't even know you! I'm not getting in the car with someone I don't know driving. Shut up and leave it alone. I'll call a cab."

"We worked together!"

"Yeah. Once. Still don't know you!"

"Twice!"

"Whatever. I'm not getting in the car!"

With that, these two strange guys in dark clothing came over and started heckling Kristina to go home with them. They said if she couldn't trust us to drive, she could trust them. Well, this just made the situation worse because Kristina didn't know them.

At this moment, I was sitting in the back seat with Melina and two other girls, and we just wanted to go home. Everyone was tired, and we really couldn't stand waiting anymore. Apparently, one of the guys bothering Kristina was getting heated with her because she wouldn't go home with them, and he told her that her personality was faker than Vanessa's breasts and lips. This was too much for Vanessa to bear. Her eyes widened, her fists tightened, and Vanessa snapped. She punched him. She began pounding on the guy and then, faster than lightening, Kristina was on him, too. The next thing I knew, Russell was pulling Vanessa off of the guy with one hand and shoving Kristina with the other. Vanessa was balling. She started to hyperventilate as the stranger in black that she attacked retreated. Russell went storming after the guy at full speed. He couldn't catch him. He tried to track him down to "beat him up," but the guy had disappeared.

Vanessa just kept crying, "My boobs are NOT fake, and so what if I get my lips injected? Everyone does!"

Russell tried to console her, "I know him. I've seen him before. He'll never work in this town, again. I'm blacklisting him with everyone I know! He'll NEVER work in this town AGAIN!"

After the shock of the fight and Russell reassuring Kristina that, "You know Malorie. She's so innocent that her father is a priest and her mother is a nun... come on!" Kristina let me drive her home.

That was the last time I saw Kristina for a long time because, just like that, she was gone to film for a hosting job, and then she was off to Connecticut for a while. My first time out without her was not pretty. I missed her. She was the only person I could talk to when we all went out. In fact, in her absence, I took on her role of being openly pissed off at everyone.

The first night that she was gone, we got a floor table at a new club. A table on the floor of the club was not my idea of paradise. We had never had one there before, and I wasn't impressed. In that situation, there are people all around you who come over and try to pick you up in the dumbest ways, even though you are at a private table. For some reason, even though I can be the sweetest person, I have no tolerance for men trying to pick me up.

One idiot came over to me, "I don't get this whole table thing."

I said, very coldly so he'd back off, "What's not to get? It's a table."

"Yeah, but is it yours? Is it for your birthday?"

"No."

"Well, then what's it for?"

"It's Russell's table. See him right there?" After pointing at Russell, I walked away, completely done with the conversation. (Don't get me wrong, I'm not a mean person, I just hate getting hit on at clubs because I'm in a committed relationship. I don't want attention from guys, and I tend to get angry when I get it. I feel that if I'm giving you no interest, you should leave. Plus, I was engaged and had a ring on my finger. In my book, that is a solid sign to leave someone alone.)

After an evening of that, we went back to the limo expecting to go back to Russell's (like always) to get our cars. Well, that didn't happen. He told the limo driver to go to some random mansion up in the hills. No one was okay with this except Vanessa and Russell (because we all had things to do the next day), but Russell didn't seem to care.

As we arrived, we noticed that it was a beautiful mansion with a great view of the valley, but no one wanted to be there. There were four of us grumbling in a corner about what we had to do the next day as 4:30am rolled around. We were pretty sure that Russell and Vanessa were having sex in different areas of the house with different people (Vanessa in one room with some girl and Russell in another room with two other women), and we were all just waiting for people who might never be ready to leave. As I gave up on fighting anyone to get back home, I began talking with another one of the deserted girls about her life. Her name was Destiny.

Destiny was one of Russell's girls who was always sweet to me. She was a little older, but she was almost like a young mother to me. She was crazy, but she took care of me (for the most part). On this night, she started spilling stories of her crazy, exciting life. At the time, I was shocked by what I had heard. Now, I know enough to know they were lies. Destiny loved to lie to make her life seem more incredible to everyone around her. I knew she was a compulsive liar when she told me that she had a boyfriend of eight years, who, through the process of abductive reasoning, I realized didn't really exist. I couldn't blame her for lying about a boyfriend; she lied about being in a relationship so Vanessa and Russell wouldn't go after her.

Destiny told me that Rebecca, another girl who was out with us, was her girlfriend. She said they were madly in love. They both had boyfriends, but the two of them were, supposedly, also in a lesbian relationship because Destiny, "can't live without being with a girl." Apparently, both of their boyfriends were okay with this, and it was known that they spent several days a week having, "girl time." I was shocked to hear this, but it was later proven to be a lie.

After listening to Destiny's stories for a while, I had had enough. I was out all night because Russell selfishly felt like stranding everyone. I started learning tricks to keep myself from being stuck out with Russell and Vanessa. I learned to have my fiancé come pick me up before we left the club with Russell so he could drive me to my car. I learned to never leave my keys in Russell's house. Russell and Vanessa got worse and worse about winding up at random locations, so my precautions became more and more handy. They would take groups of girls to large "after parties," and then the girls would be stranded. They would also leave girls at the clubs if they were ready to leave and didn't see them. So, always have a backup to get home when you go out with the "Russell types." I had learned my lesson, and, with Kristina gone, I found myself distancing from Russell a lot. She was the catalyst to keep me around them, and, with her gone, I found myself unmotivated to be around that trashy group of people. I was working hard to afford my rent and acting tools. Headshots were expensive, as were keeping my casting profiles updated. Why was I wasting my valuable free time with Russell? I could be at home relaxing. Was he really capable of helping me at all? I really did try to be friends with them, but they were too slimy to be true friends with. I wasn't sure how much longer I could keep up appearances with them without Kristina around.

# Getting to Know Destiny

Despite the fact that I hadn't gotten into a Playboy Mansion party for months, I still hung around with Russell with the hope that, maybe, someone he knew could get me in. (Though it seemed silly of me to stay around, I was a surprisingly naïve and hopeful person.) There was also a part of me that hung around out of some strange sense of responsibility or familiarity. It was something that didn't make sense, but it kept me feeling like I had to stay. Regardless, through these later escapades with Russell, I got to know Destiny, the compulsive liar. The first event that brought us closer together took place when we thought we were going to a concert. I was told that we were going to be backstage. Before we left, when I got to Russell's place, there were at least 35 girls there. We all got in different cars, but I demanded to be in the back seat of Russell's car, as I didn't know these other girls. The location of the concert was close to two hours away, and I got incredibly sick riding in the back seat of Russell's car as he sped to make it in time. He went 90 miles per hour down the freeway, swerving in and out of cars the entire way. This made me doubt my decision of wanting to be in his car. What was I thinking? Not to mention, one of the girls invited another Playboy office employee to the event. Russell was furious. The whole car ride he complained that she could never come with them again. He would get fired if she saw him doing drugs or having sex with the girls. He claimed that this would ruin his whole weekend. He got a hotel (which he dubbed a "VIP suite") for everyone to stay at if they wanted to, but I knew that a "VIP suite" probably wasn't good news. I made arrangements to get a ride with Destiny or to have Damian pick me up so I wouldn't get stuck again.

As everyone made a pit stop at the hotel to drop off their luggage, I got in Destiny's car to head up to the concert. We got there only to find out that it was NOT a concert. Everyone was pissed, including Russell, because the guy who got him in did not tell him that it was a rave! There were naked people, crazy colors, and techno music as far as the eye could see. It was definitely a rave. I had never seen anyone naked in public before, and I was appalled.

Destiny and I wouldn't drink (anything at all-not even the soda) because they brought alcohol and soda in in water bottles, so it wouldn't be confiscated. They tore the labels off and just hid what they could. Unsealed drinks without labels were definitely something you wanted to stay away from. We were not chancing getting drugged.

For the majority of the night, Destiny followed me around and told me crazy stories about her and her "girlfriend" Rachel. We never really talked with Rachel, who was there, but, when she was more than 10 feet away from Destiny, it seemed Destiny would have a panic attack. At midnight, I was listening to Destiny murmur on and on when I witnessed something horrible happen. Two girls had gotten drunk while dancing on the stage. One of them lunged at the other and started making out with her. She forced her friend to the edge of the stage with her embrace. Within seconds, they tumbled off the stage. The girl who initiated flipped over her friend and her friend fell head first onto the pavement. The poor girl cracked her head open on the cement. The ambulance came immediately after, and Destiny and I left after seeing that the girl was safely moved to the hospital. Luckily, Destiny got me back safely to Damian that night.

The next big night I had with Destiny was on *Cinco de Mayo*. We went for a *Cinco de Mayo* celebration at the Roosevelt Hotel in Hollywood to hear LMFAO play. We got there before the event began, surprisingly! We started out with about 15 girls. When we piled out of the limo and went to the gate, they had to drag us in through the crowd after a minute or two of waiting. Because we were a lot of girls pushing through, other people starting tugging on us and pushing us, trying to go with us. The girls started pushing on me as I went in the gate, and they slammed my arm against the corner of the fence and pushed. My arm was close to being snapped in two, so I screamed and let go of the girl in front of me. It was incredibly painful, but, luckily, I managed to pull my arm out of position and get through in one piece. Once we got through the gate, we had to walk past the line to get into the pool area. As we walked by girls waiting to get in, they began to get angry. One girl stuck her nose up at us. "Why the hell do they get to cut? What the hell?" she started yelling at us. I felt bad because I really didn't want to be there in the crowds with Russell and his girls. I craved to be with my fiancé. I missed him when we were parted for more than a few hours. Why did I get to be here cutting the lines while girls who really wanted it were left behind? I didn't understand. It didn't seem fair.

As we were walking into the event, Emma, one of the girls, tried to amuse everyone by asking, "Who's had sex in an elevator?"

Melina replied, "I have."

I held back a giggle.

Emma narrowed her eyes, "Really!? Have you joined the mile-high club?"

"Yeah."

I couldn't help but produce an audible laugh at Melina. Who wouldn't have expected that? I tried to hide my chuckles, but her gaze caught mine. Fortunately, she was a little too oblivious to realize that I was laughing at her.

Once we were successful in passing the violent crowds, we got to sit at the tables, which turned out to be a bunch of fluffy, outdoor beach chairs pulled together to create one giant pillow. It made sense, as the party was out by the pool of the hotel. I sat with Destiny and her friend Emma and we began talking. My whole evening was basically spent talking to Destiny. She was trying to pick me up, and I was onto her tricks. The one thing she wasn't lying about was being bisexual.

Destiny sat next to me on the same poolside chair, staring intently into my eyes. She was practically whispering to me, "So... as far as guys and girls go, I have amazingly high standards. I told you that my guy lets me sleep with any girl I want, right? You see, girls aren't cheating. Does your fiancé let you sleep with girls?"

I looked at her a little suspiciously, "No. In my relationship, cheating is cheating... no matter who it's with. Damian knows that if I had sex with anyone else, it would be because I had feelings for them, so that's not okay."

Destiny smiled, "You're just so innocent and adorable, and I love that. You know, I would have sex with three people at this party. Well, obviously, you're one of them. You are so gorgeous. I have a little crush on you."

As Destiny moved closer to me, I started scooting back slightly.

"I'd also have sex with Melina because she's so exotic. Also Emma. In fact, Emma is coming home with me tonight to hook up after the party. We've pre-planned it. We both want to have some fun! You know, I think Vanessa is pretty enough to have sex with, but she's done way too much with way too many people for me to want to touch her." I smiled at the irony that she wanted to sleep with Melina but not Vanessa because she thought she had been around too much.

At this time we watched Russell, Vanessa, Melina, and their herd of bimbos go up into a "special VIP area," which wound up being some guys' hotel room where they were going to do drugs. Emma filtered out with them leaving Destiny and I alone.

Destiny and I stayed outside talking. She began telling me a story, and, each second into it, she leaned closer and closer into me. "I traveled to Cambodia last year, and I was bit by a mosquito. It gave me the 'vampire disease.' It's real! It's not like you see on TV where you suck blood and live in a coffin, but the vampire stories are really based off of this vampire disease. This disease killed me for three seconds. I had to get brought back to life! It killed me and brought me back like a vampire. Now, I'm pale, allergic to garlic, and am able to give people energy. I can control them and make them do what I want."

I blankly stared at her, knowing that she was prone to lies. She was not fazed by my look, "I want to show you that this is true. I will touch anyone right now and transfer lust to them. I'll make them want me. Let's do this!"

Suddenly, Emma busted in between us. She was crying. She began huffing a story to us about how LMFAO, the group playing, were all in the VIP room with her and Russell. She said that they were jerks. When she knocked into one of them, he told her that she was ugly and to get out, so she was crying and calling them all "Faggots" every two seconds. Destiny would talk, and then Emma would cut in with, "They were so mean!"

This played right into Destiny's plan. To console her, Destiny touched Emma's arms and massaged them or, as she called it, "transferred her energy to her." Emma stopped crying and became turned on. It was at this moment when Destiny made out with her. When Destiny pulled away, Emma began violently going after Destiny for more, then went all over other people as if a chain reaction. "See?" Destiny asked.

She turned back to me and leaned in with her forehead almost touching mine, "I want to do it to you. Let me kiss you."

I glared at her, and she moved in so her forehead was touching mine. I replied, "I can't."

She backed away, clearly a little irritated. She was putting her efforts into seducing me, and I wasn't having it, "Oh, right. The cheating thing." She rolled her eyes.

From that moment on, she spent the whole night with me, making sure that I was near her. She'd brush up against me every few minutes and grab my shoulders. It was funny, but annoying. Then, she began to dance. She started swaying seductively against this random girl's boyfriend, and he just went with her, bellowing, "It's like she's trying to seduce me!"

Then, another guy came over and asked her out, and she gave him her number. (This was, of course, another sign that she didn't have a boyfriend of eight years.)

Russell asked, "What about your boyfriend?"

"We're not married," she chuckled.

Having deciphered her lies, what I did know about Destiny was that she liked me. I also knew that she liked to have sex with girls, and that she dated guys. She claimed that people were drawn to her because of the vampire disease, which made her produce sexual energy to transfer to people. What that really meant was that she was good at seducing people. I was sure she knew how to radiate her energy. In Michael Chekhov acting training, we learned how to "radiate our energy." It's the same thing as "smiling with your eyes" in modeling. It makes your presence stand out and pull for attention. It's stage presence. She has it, and she knows how to use it to get people to pay attention to her. I think that's the true secret of what she calls her "vampire disease."

That night was weird and tiring. By the end of it, I was exhausted. Everyone else went back to the room, and I sat out in the hall with Destiny, exasperated. There were jasmine flowers blooming around outside, and I loved them because they smelled like honeysuckles. So, I picked them and put some in my hair. It transported me back to my childhood. There are honeysuckles all around my home in Virginia, and I would eat the honey out of them as a kid. We had them in my backyard. Going back to that place in my mind, I couldn't help but let go and be happy. I tried to hold my attention to the beautiful jasmine flowers over all the ridiculousness that was occurring. I didn't even pretend to drink that night. I was too tired, and that whole situation with Destiny was funny. I went back to Damian laughing about the silly seduction that Destiny tried to pull.

# The Invitation:
# The Day My Fate Changed for the Best

It had been close to a year that I had been hanging out with Russell, but it felt like much longer. I still hadn't stepped foot on the cobblestone paths of the Playboy Mansion. I was losing hope just as quickly as I was losing patience with Russell and his bimbos. The drama was getting to me, as was hanging around with Destiny during Kristina's absence. What was left for me to do here? I was lost. I knew full well what Russell was about, and I had no hope that he could introduce me to anyone real within Playboy. I was ready to walk away and take back my free time.

Just before I had lost the last drop of my hope, I met someone that pushed me to where I wanted to be. Her name was Alicia. Alicia and I worked together on a shoot. Funny enough, I actually met her through Russell, so, inadvertently, Russell did wind up helping me in the end. That was never his intention, but he did. Alicia and I hit it off, immediately. During the shoots that I had with her and over a few outings with Russell, Alicia and I stuck together. We were both distant from the other girls, and one of our IQs was probably higher than ten of the other girls' IQs combined. After speaking with Alicia for several days, she told me stories of how she visited the Playboy Mansion every weekend. She said that she was dating Hef's nephew, Morgan, and that it was quite complicated. She began telling me all the crazy stories of their escapades, and I did nothing more than listen to them and wonder how she made it to the Playboy Mansion—not just at a party, but as a dinner guest. I guess it was through her relationship with Morgan?

One night, Alicia pulled me aside and said, "You really want to go to the Playboy Mansion, don't you?"

I glared at her with wide eyes, "I really, really do."

"Okay," she replied, "I don't EVER do this, but, for some reason, I really like you. I feel like you're more than an average girl and I think you're one of the few people I've met that could wind up being a Playmate one day. I want to invite you to go to the Playboy Mansion."

"Are you serious?"

"Yes. I'm going to get you in touch with Hef's secretary. Just say who you are, that I invited you, and tell them about yourself. Also, please send pictures to her in your email." She gave me the email to the woman in the office at the Playboy Mansion.

"Thank you so much!" I couldn't believe her generosity.

As soon as I arrived home, I composed an email to Hef's secretary. I included my information, how I was associated with Playboy, some of my modeling portfolio, and a little biography about myself. Not even a day had passed before she responded to me. She said that Hef would love to have me come up for a movie night. I stared at my email in shock. I couldn't believe it. My dream had come true! She told me that I was welcome to come on a Friday, Saturday, or Sunday of my choosing. I was to let her know, and she'd add me to the list.

I shot up out of my chair and danced around upon reading her email. I ran to Damian to tell him the news. He knew this was something I had dreamed of since I was a teenager watching *The Girls Next Door* with him and he couldn't have been happier for me. I really appreciated him for that. (Thankfully, he always supported this dream of mine, and he loved using the fact that I hung out at the Playboy Mansion for bragging rights, of course.)

The question that still lingers in my mind today is, "What made Hef say yes to me?" There were so many girls I knew from the Mansion that tried to get other girls invited up and Hef would not allow it. This happened in a time when they were inviting less people, and most of the girls I knew got up because of who they knew, not out of chance. But something made him say yes to me, and I am so appreciative of it. His decision to invite me changed my life forever.

# Looking Back On Russell

Knowing what I know now, there are a lot of negative things I could say about Russell. Russell truly was the epitome of everything that is wrong with Hollywood. He preyed on young girls that were new to Hollywood off of amateur modeling sites. He used the fact that he casted for *Playboy TV* to lure in unsuspecting girls and then took advantage of them. He tricked so many people into having threesomes with him and his girlfriend, and they got nothing out of it in return. He tarnished the Playboy name by treating people this way while going out, and then parading around saying, "We're with Playboy! We're representing Playboy." If Playboy Enterprises ever knew that he was taking large groups of girls out and giving them drugs and trying to have sex with them while saying it was a "Playboy outing," he would have been instantly fired. At least, I hope he would have been.

It was even more torturous for me to have to go out with him and his crew knowing this and watching him snake around these women. I tried to help the girls that needed help, but most of them did not want to be helped. I am a kind person who tries to help everyone, and I had no business being around him. But, I treated my endeavors with him like work. I was going to these events to get somewhere that I wanted to be. And, luckily, in the end, through no direct help of his own, Russell did get me where I wanted to be.

I learned, later, about the unspoken hierarchy that Playboy had. (This was before Playboy and Playboy Plus became two different vehicles.) Throughout my time with him, Russell was on the lowest tier of the company. *Playboy TV* was the lowest of the low, and a lot of it was just plain porn. I say that it is the lowest part of Playboy because most people didn't take it seriously. That was where Russell was, and he barely even deserved to be there. I'm sad to say that Russell wound up getting promoted, and I'm even sadder to say that Russell never got caught in what he was doing. Some girls tried to rat him out for the things that he did, but he would blacklist them and immediately block them so they couldn't publicly show what he had done. He hid who his bosses were so well that no one could really touch him.

As I got more involved at the Playboy Mansion, I found that the important people in Hef's life knew nothing of Russell or what he was doing. In fact, they knew nothing about *Playboy TV* or Playboy Plus or anything that went on there. Russell could get away with these things because the upper tier of the unspoken Playboy hierarchy was so oblivious to the underworking. Russell would always just be a snake in the fields of the Playboy spectrum.

At this point, I had no real reason to be around Russell anymore. This pseudo "best friend" position to him and Vanessa was graining on my sanity, and Kristina had still not returned from her trips on the East Coast. She was the only person who made them manageable to me. My tolerance for dealing with him had evaporated, and I was disgusted more than ever by his actions toward a lot of these aspiring young models he seemed to seduce. However, I couldn't help but feel bad for dropping him out of my life. As a gesture of kindness, I continued to see Russell and his girls for the next few months. My relationship with him overlapped with my endeavors at the Playboy Mansion, slightly, until they slowly dissolved away. Even currently we aren't enemies, but I definitely caused some waves with him and his crew, and some drama splashed out of these waves over time. At this point, though, I didn't care about them at all. I was so lucky to be where I was. In my mind, the Playboy Mansion was the true essence of Playboy, and it was quite sad to look back at the illusion that Russell painted. How sad that little illusion really was.

MALORIE MACKEY

# Part 2:
# The Routine of the Playboy Mansion

MALORIE MACKEY

# My First Trip to the Playboy Mansion

It was set! Officially, I was invited to a Playboy Mansion Movie Night. I was ecstatic. Upon receiving my invitation, I texted Alicia a thank you message.

She replied, "Anytime. I only like to help people that make an impression, and I feel like you deserve it. You'll have so much fun and really get in good with Playboy, much more than these other girls."

I wanted to share this experience with Alicia, especially since she knew how to get there, where to go, where to sit, and all the ins and outs. Unfortunately, at the time, she lived in Arizona and was going to be spending the next half of the year back there. So, I had to go to the Playboy Mansion for the first time by myself.

As I began preparing for my trip to the Mansion, I reflected back on the last year. It had almost been a full year since we arrived on the west coast. Time was really flying by, but things were going well. I was frequently auditioning, Damian was learning the ins and outs of Indie filmmaking, and we were still very happy with our apartment. And, now, I had accomplished my dream of getting invited to the Mansion. Things were looking up, and we were happily living the life that we wanted in Los Angeles.

Luckily, at this time, I still worked for Victoria's Secret. It was my favorite place online to shop for clothing, so most of my wardrobe came from there. Because of that, I had a great selection of clothes to choose from for my first trip up to the Playboy Mansion. (I had much better attire to choose from this time around. Nothing like that Russell embarrassment with the pink leopard top would happen again.)

I spent the entire week before my visit picking out a nice lace top and boots as I anxiously waited for the 20th to come around. I went to extreme lengths the week before to ensure that I would make a good first impression. I did my nails, got a spray tan, and had my hair done. I had no idea what it was going to be like, but I was going to be dressed to impress! (I'm not usually very fashion forward, so this was something that I really had to try for.)

Finally, the day came for my first movie night. As I was driving there, I discovered that the closer I got to the Mansion, the more nervous I became. I began to doubt myself. I didn't know how to act or what to do. So, I called Destiny, who claimed that she had visited the Playboy Mansion several times with Corey Feldman, who she used to be friends with. Destiny did not help, at all. In fact, she made the situation much worse. She told me a whirlpool of lies, which, inevitably, made me sick.

I picked up the phone, "Destiny. I'm on my way to the Mansion. Do you have any advice for me?"

"Yes! I definitely have advice for you," she said. "If Hef tries to give you pajamas to wear, keep the top on, and that means that you don't want sex."

(That was a flat out lie. There is no sex at movie night, and he does not give anyone pajamas there. This lie developed from stories of him having sex with girlfriends before, and that has nothing to do with movie night guests. Regardless, from all angles, it was inaccurate.)

"The girls who have been there the longest get the best bean bags to sit on during the movie."

(That answer was misinformed as well. There are sofas and chairs in Hef's living room that face a movie screen for everyone to watch the movie. There are cushions set up in front of Hef's couch as well, right by the screen, for guests to lay on to watch the movie. Yes, those basically get claimed by regulars, but they are not bean bags, and, on Friday nights, they are almost always up for grabs.)

"Also, he loves to give out a sort of powder substance that goes in your drink. Don't take it. It's powdered E, and it's supposed to make you horny."

(Again, in terms of movie nights, this was a flat out lie based on stories of the past.)

"If you get on the trampoline, your top comes off!"

*(At this point she was absolutely making this stuff up.)*

You can imagine how horrified I was. It was at that moment that I truly realized how much I was still the same old Malorie. After all my endeavors with Russell, after all that I had seen, I was still afraid of the unknown. I believed her for a second and felt as if I was going right back into a Russell story. I was afraid that I was in over my head going to the Mansion now. I wanted to hyperventilate. My excited, nervous energy turned sour, and I got a big nasty pit in my stomach. Regardless, visiting the Mansion was a dream, along with meeting Hugh Hefner, and I was going to make that happen. I hung up with Destiny and pulled up to the gate at the front of the property, which happened to be closed. I was told to look for an intercom and to give security my name through that device. I looked everywhere, and I couldn't see it. I'm sure I looked like an idiot scanning my eyes down the front of the gate, to the bushes, and then to the ground.

Suddenly, I heard a voice coming from a rock. My confused look dissolved as I realized that the intercom was discretely placed in a large rock to the left of the driveway right by my driver-side window. They asked for my name, and, once given my name, they confirmed that I was on their list. Those large, Victorian gates began to part, as if in slow motion, and I started up the long driveway. The gates to the Playboy Mansion opened before me, and my dream was unfolding before my eyes.

The driveway to the Playboy Mansion seemed to stretch on for days. On the way up, there was a traffic sign that said "Playmates at Play." Upon ascending up the long road, if you looked to your left, you could see the side of the Mansion beautifully lit with pastel colors.

Once I arrived to the loop in front of the house, the valet took my car. I stood there for a second looking blankly around. *What do I do? The valet just took my car, and I'm standing at the front door of the Playboy Mansion. Do I walk in? They don't just let you walk right in the front door of the Playboy Mansion, do they?* I looked around, confused for a second. No one else was around...so I walked in, and to my surprise, it was empty. I stepped into the giant entry hall with the great staircase off to my immediate left. Ahead of me there was an entrance to a bar on the porch, and behind me was a collection of pictures of Hef on the wall, along with a portrait of Hef, Crystal (his fiancé at the time), and their dog Charlie. To my right there was an entrance into two separate dining rooms and the kitchen, plus there was a table which had pictures from previous movie nights stored away in envelopes on it. I found out that they document and scrapbook the events and place the extra pictures out for people to grab. At this moment, I was lucky enough to be greeted by the photographer who took several photos of me for the scrapbook, too. He snapped a few photos before heading over into the kitchen, leaving me to continue wandering.

For a few minutes I just wandered and looked, and I was the only person in the Mansion besides the staff. Was I really that early? I examined a lot of the fine art pictures scattered around the walls. (There was one in particular that had a cigarette burn on it that I later found out was put there by John Lennon.) Then, the front door opened, and in walked an older blonde woman. You could tell that she used to be very pretty, and that she definitely had money because she had quite a bit of plastic surgery done. Her old-style lip implants were quite noticeable. Fortunately, she was so sweet and welcoming. She was a bundle of energy. She saw me and came running over.

This was Roberta. She was not shy, and that was just what I needed at this moment, someone to talk with and open me up. I held the door to the outdoor bar open for her, and she said, "I always feel good when I have a beautiful woman hold the door open for me!" She led me around, showed me the bar, showed me the dining room, and started speaking with me. At this moment, it was just her, a young model who was clearly a centerfold, and an older gentleman there in the Mansion with us. I had no idea who these people were, but I would soon know them all very well.

Roberta showed me where I could sit along the large main dining table. She, first, asked me if I was at the Mansion testing for centerfold. From then on, every person I met in the Mansion (aside from Hef) asked me the same thing. I took this as a good sign. If they thought that, then they must think I was pretty.

This nice woman talked all of us into being the first to attack the buffet table. She sat down next to me and another dark-haired woman who had come in. We sat at the far end of the large, elliptical main table of the dining room. When she introduced me to the dark-haired woman she said, "Isn't she beautiful?"

The dark-haired woman added, "Yes. Something stands out about her."

"Is it the eyes?"

"I think so. They're so bright."

It was so nice of them. I didn't know what to expect, but I sure wasn't planning on meeting such wonderful ladies. For dinner we ate salad, fruits, soup, salmon, rice, and asparagus. There was also a buffet of coffee, tea, cookies, and cakes. Everything was absolutely phenomenal.

Then I was introduced to an extremely nice and outgoing couple who also happened to be from Virginia. Joel Berliner and Alison Reynolds were a perfectly kind older couple, and Joel grew up near where I did in Midlothian, Virginia. They were immediately nice to me. We spoke for the longest time about Virginia, and they wanted to know all about me and what I did. They were a very bright and attractive couple who seemed to look better with age. I found out later that Alison used to be one of Hef's social secretaries in the '70s, and the couple tended to have quite a strong influence on Hef. They were the nicest people you could find at the Mansion, and they made everyone feel welcomed. They truly made me feel right at home on my first trip. (They were more or less Hef's welcoming committee, as they were generally always the first to greet everyone.)

Roberta asked me how I got invited to the Mansion. I explained my story thus far, in minor details, including my college degree, and she told me that she also had a BFA in performance. She was a soap opera star who did a lingerie addition of Playboy. She was invited many years ago, but she was too scared of what would happen at the Mansion, so she turned it down. Her friend finally convinced her to go one day, and she was shocked at how fun and innocent it was. She was always shy, though, and Hef finally approached her one day and asked why she was so quiet every time. She'd been comfortable ever since.

So far, it seemed that it was just a normal dinner with a group of good friends. Everyone was so kind, and everyone was very open to new faces. Sitting down with these people I felt that I had known them for years, even though it had, truly, only been minutes. It was nice to feel so welcomed. I also noticed that the only young people at this dinner were me and the centerfold that I mentioned before. Her name was Olivia Paige, and she was living at the Bunny House at the time. She, too, was incredibly nice to me and I got along with her well.

Then, as if I was having a dream, Hugh Hefner entered the room. I went from having fun to being scared all over again. He sat down at the head of the table, across from the area of the table I was at. I wasn't used to seeing celebrities, and I didn't know how to act. I wasn't used to this lifestyle yet. Hugh Hefner was sitting at the same table as me. He occasionally looked my way and noticed me, which really made me feel gracious, yet more nervous.

Finally, Joel leaned over to me, "Have you met Hef yet?"

My eyes widened, "Not yet."

"Well, let's go!"

Suddenly, Joel had my arm and was pulling me out of the seat. He led me the fifteen steps it took to get to the head of the table to Hef, but it felt as if we had walked for miles. He tapped Hef on the shoulder and said, "Hey Hef! This is Malorie. This is her first time here. I wanted to introduce you. Isn't she pretty?"

Hugh Hefner looked me in the eyes, shook my hand, and said, "Yes. Hi."

My mind blanked. I didn't know what to say for a second. The only words that I could muster were, "Nice to meet you. Thanks for having me here as a guest."

He then averted his attention back to Crystal, his fiancé, who was sitting next to him along with Anna Sophia Berglund, another girl that lived at the Mansion.

Now, before I came here, I was warned not to talk to him if he didn't approach me, so I went back over to my chair. Rumor had it that Crystal was very protective of him, so we could only talk to him if someone else initiated it, as is what happened with me. So, because Joel was so kind, I got to meet Hef.

I officially met Hugh Hefner. How surreal.

Joel looked back at me as we sat down in our seats, "So, this is it. There's usually ten to fifteen people here on Friday and Saturday, and then thirty to forty on Sunday. That's it. Different than you expected, huh?"

So...after all the rumors about "the Playboy Mansion" and all the craziness...the sex...the drugs...the girls....it all turned out to be lies and rumors left behind from the chaos of the 1970s. Do you know what modern-day movie nights at the Mansion were? They were a bunch of old friends getting together, having dinner, and watching old movies. They just all happened to be in the industry or related to Hugh Hefner. It was nice, friendly, and fun. And it was comfortable—nothing like what I had heard.

Like clockwork, at 6:30pm we all piled into the movie room to watch the movie "Out of Sight" with George Clooney. We sat down in the beautifully designed space, which was a living room converted with a screen. Hef sat with Crystal and Anna on the first couch, and then people piled on the couches elevated behind him while some sat on the floor on pillows. I sat on a chair next to Hef's couch. The movie was decent, but

I couldn't get over the fact that I was sitting next to Hef's couch the whole night.

After the movie, we gathered in the Great Hall for finger sandwiches, cookies, and tea. I said goodbye to all the older people that I had met. The centerfold peeled out during the movie because she was starting a burlesque class that she had to go to. So, while I was drinking my tea, I got to speak with a girl testing for centerfold that snuck in near the end of the movie. She had been approved and was waiting to see if her actual centerfold shoot was good enough to earn a month. She had been "stuck" in the guest house at the Mansion alone for a few weeks, and she wanted to get out. After asking, I found out this was Amanda Cerny. We agreed to stay in touch, though, we never really became good friends.

As I left the Mansion grounds, all of the shrubbery and fountains were lit up beautifully, and there were green and purple lights shining on the building, making it look like a castle. It was almost ethereal. I took in a deep breath full of crisp, evening air and cherished this moment. After everything sunk in, I drove away hoping that I would soon be back for another movie night.

My wish was granted, and I was invited back to the Playboy Mansion the following weekend.

This next time that I went back, it was the same story. We had great food, nice company, and we watched "A Face in the Crowd" with Andy Griffith. I loved that movie. It was incredibly intense and sad, but it made a great point about the media that is still true today. For the first time, I laid down by Hef and Crystal's feet on the cushions up front. You see, they set up bed-like cushions on the floor like a nice, reclined seat, and I got to be up front right in the middle of the screen, which provided a perfect view. I got to speak to Hef a little this time, because Crystal wasn't really around. He was very sweet. The whole thing was so much fun. I met more people, and I was planning on coming soon to attend my first *Fun in the Sun* and the screening of "The Hangover Part II."

This movie ordeal was turning into a weekly event, and I loved it. Unlike the rendezvous with Russell and Vanessa, I really, truly enjoyed the movie nights. What's not to enjoy about hanging around, talking with good people, eating amazing food, and watching classic movies? It was my cup of tea, and I did not want to miss out on it. As I mentioned before, I was a homebody. I hated partying and everything involved with it. For the first time, my involvement with Playboy allowed me to be myself. I could enjoy things that I liked for a change, and no one was telling me how to dress or how to act, like Russell and Vanessa did. I was free to be who I was. Not to mention, the room was always filled with great producers, directors, and legends. Who wouldn't enjoy that?

# A Typical Movie Night

Before I continue, there is something that you must know about Hugh Hefner. Hef lives by routine. Every week he has the exact same schedule. He will eat the same things on the same days, organize the same weekly events, and nothing can be different. For instance, Monday nights were always "Manly Nights," where just the men came together to order food and watch a movie. Tuesday nights were game nights with Hef and the girls living at the Bunny House. Thursday Nights were more intimate movie nights. Then, the big, eventful movie nights were on Friday, Saturday, and Sunday. The Playboy Mansion was a giant routine.

It wasn't long before I, officially, became a regular at the Playboy Mansion, and I attended movie nights one, two, or three times per weekend. (I was able to go whenever I pleased on a Friday, Saturday, or a Sunday. If I didn't, this book wouldn't be very interesting.) I'm going to take this time to outline a normal movie night for you. Friday and Saturday nights were the general, classic movie nights, while Sundays were *Fun in the Sun* (or FITS) Sundays. I'll tell you about that later.

On a Friday or Saturday movie night, one would show up at 5pm. You always pulled up to the gate, got approved by security, and made that long drive up the driveway. At the top of the hill the valet would take your car, then you walked through that big, wooden door into the Mansion. Naturally, once you go a certain number of times, you develop your own routine, too. I was no different. I would always walk in, head straight for the movie room, and put my purse down on the first set of cushions up front. As I mentioned, there were four piles of cushions for guests to lay on in front of Hef's couch. Richard (Dickie) Bann, an old friend of Hef's, always took the first set of cushions to the far left (if you are looking at the screen). He set them up the perfect way to comfortably watch the movie, and no one could take his spot. The spot next to Richard's became Alicia's spot for a long time (the girl that got me into the Mansion) once she finally moved to LA from Arizona. For a while, while she was in Arizona, no one sat there. Then, there was a pile of cushions that was usually empty unless someone random was visiting. Finally, the cushions all the way to the right and closest to the door were mine. (It was a strategic move on my part because I had to use the restroom many times during a movie. Being the closest cushions to the door, I could easily roll over and slip out of the movie room.)

Next, I would go out to the great hall and get my photo taken by the scrapbook photographers. (I would like to address the scrapbooking photos quickly. I have heard, recently, that people have come out saying that they were a form of abuse, because you had to take photos and see your imperfections every day. I think this is ridiculous. Hef has kept scrapbooks as a hobby his whole life. The fact that he offers his guests photos from each visit is a nice gesture, I think. It's a way for you to collect your own memories at the Mansion, and I love finding photos that I had forgotten I had taken weeks later. If you are secure in yourself as a person and don't care how others view you, then you will enjoy finding photos taken of you—not feel insecure by them.)

I would then go out to the bartender, who always had my Shirley Temple made when he saw me. From there, I went in and claimed my spot at the main dinner table.

There were several tables you could choose to sit at during movie night dinner. There was the long, main dining table and a small circular table in the main dining room. In the Mediterranean room next to the dining room, there was another small table. Lastly, there was a small, circular table back in a cold, stone room that was hidden away. That one was, mostly, left vacant. I always sat at the large, main table in the dining room. That was the only table that had some assigned seats. The head of the table closest to the dining room's entrance was where Hef sat. The seats to his left and right were always reserved for girlfriends. The seat next to the girlfriends', on one side, was for Ray Anthony and, on the other side, was for Richard Bann, Hef's dearest and oldest friends. Then, the two seats next to Ray were for Keith (Hef's brother) and Caya (Keith's girlfriend and later his wife). Next to Caya sat Alicia, and I sat next to Alicia, which happened to be the seat next to the other head of the table. The other head chair, for a long time, was left for Alison Reynolds. Joel sat next to Alison, and the few empty seats next to Joel were, generally, up for grabs or taken by Playmate Ava Fabian or Hef's old social secretary, Cis Rundle.

We would spend 5pm - 6:30pm chatting about our weeks and helping ourselves to a lovely dinner buffet consisting of fruit, salads, broccoli, bread, tomatoes, some type of soup or stew, vegetable or rice sides, a seafood option, a chicken option, and a beef option. There were always three choices for dessert and all the coffee and tea we could want. Plus, the bar was always open. It was amazing. We would also use this time to go through the scrapbook photos that Hef left out and take copies that he made for us.

Hef wouldn't come down and join anyone until about 6pm. (And the older he got, the later he would wait to come down.) His girlfriends and he would always come down late to the dinner, having eaten upstairs, and join the last bits of conversation before the movie. Then, at 6:30pm sharp, Hef would arise from his seat at the table and announce, "It's movie time," and we'd all filter into the living room for the movie. Hef's couch was the first one in front of the screen. He'd sit there with his girlfriends. I already mentioned the cushions in front of his sofa. There was a second couch directly behind Hef's set up for Ray Anthony, Keith, and Caya. There were tons of folding chairs placed all around for the other guests. The staff set up the chairs and cushions each night for each movie and then removed them once the movie was over. I felt bad that they had to keep putting up the setup and taking it down. One night I tried to help, but they told me that they would get in trouble for allowing guests to help clean up. So, I never tried that again.

The Friday movies always started with Hef sitting up on the edge of his sofa and reading special notes about the movie's history. The movie notes were written by Richard Bann and consisted of five minutes or so of interesting facts about the movie and its making. Then, a cartoon (usually Looney Tunes) set to the theme of the movie would play, followed by the movie itself. We would watch classics from the 30s, 40s, 50s, 60s, and 70s. It was a stream of the best films of all time. I have to say, I learned so much about classic film from Hugh Hefner. Unfortunately, as he began to get older, the movie notes stopped happening, but the movies kept playing until the end of my time there. At 86 and 87 years old, Hef had no problem reading the notes clearly. Once he reached 88 into 89 years old, he began stumbling on words, which is, probably, why the notes were removed. I still miss listening to Hef brief us before the movies on fun facts and histories of the movies we watched. (After all, I've always enjoyed history.)

Unlike most of the girls, I loved the classic movies. Yes, some were boring, but the majority were wonderful. I loved the old costumes, the old styling, and the classic makeup. I loved the way the women used to speak. In fact, it made me wish I lived in the past. Film in the 40s and 50s had such a wit about it that no media has now. Everyone was more complex, and their responses were more deep and detailed. "Bonnie and Clyde," "Streetcar Named Desire," "Blood and Sand," "Some Like It Hot," and "The Bride of Frankenstein" all became favorites of mine. I fell in love with Humphrey Bogart and Alfred Hitchcock, and I learned that my classic movie doppelganger was Lee Remick. (Everyone told me how much I looked like her after we watched a few of her old movies. I would walk into dinner and Joel would say, "Well, if it isn't Lee Remick..." I was in Heaven.) Not to mention, I have Obsessive Compulsive Disorder, so I was actually a fan of the routine in place. Most of the girls I spoke with would go crazy doing the same things all the time, but I enjoyed it immensely.

After the movies, we would go out in the great hall, again, for sandwiches (with the crust cut off, of course), tea, coffee, and cookies. Then, everyone would slowly filter out at about 9pm, if not before.

There were a few nights where some of the girls and I would be stressed out, so we'd go back and relax in the grotto for an hour before leaving the grounds. We were welcome to stay on the grounds and swim, go to the gym, tan, hang out, and talk until around 11pm if we really wanted to stay. Sometimes we took advantage of that. Most of the times, however, we'd leave once the movie was over. Whenever we did take advantage of the grotto on those late nights after the movies, I would stop and pull myself out of reality for a second. I'd listen to the gentle splashing of the water outside of the grotto. I would take the time to acknowledge where I was and appreciate it while I had it. I would tell my friends, "Let's really enjoy this time. Who knows when it may end." All I can say now is that I'm glad I took that time for myself. I was truly blessed, and I appreciated where I was and what the universe had gifted me. In a time when I could barely feed myself at home and was just getting settled into the expenses of living in LA, I had a place with, not only amazing free meals, but a place where I was considered family. Since my husband and I had no family out in LA, it was a magical thing to find. It was a surreal experience that I fully appreciated.

# The Guests

Since the Mansion was all about routine, the regulars that surrounded Hef in his daily life were mostly people who had been by his side for years. They became part of the routine and always adjusted their lives to the schedule that Hef created.

First, there was Hef's brother, Keith. Keith was a wonderful man. He was kind-hearted, always talking to everyone, and he looked very good for his age. Keith worked out and played tennis often, so he was, naturally, in great shape. (Later on, his girlfriend would stress how controlling and jealous he was, but this was a side of Keith that I never saw first-hand. I always thought that he was nothing but kind.)

Keith's lovely girlfriend (and later bride), Caya, was always good friends with whomever Hef's main girlfriend was. Her loyalty was connected to a spot at the table and not, necessarily, to an individual. She was a beautiful Indonesian girl with a very strong accent. She was kind, but you always had to be careful not to say the wrong thing to her. Again, she seemed to be the property of Hef's number-one girlfriend rather than a true individual. I didn't blame her for that, though. If she had to be around the Mansion every day, why not get along with the people living there? Caya was always nice to me, and I liked her a lot.

Ray Anthony was one of Hef's oldest friends. Ray was a famous band leader from back in the day. He was famous for his recording of "The Bunny Hop," and he played a mean trumpet. I had the pleasure of hearing him play, first hand, on a couple of occasions. He was definitely a hound dog, and he used to work with Marilyn Monroe. Even though he was in his 90s, in my prime at the Mansion, that didn't stop him from flocking to all the ladies. He would flirt and use the fact that he was a cute old man to get pictures with all of the girls. He was a player in the body of a harmless old man. But, it was all in good fun. Those who liked *The Girls Next Door* will remember Ray Anthony very well.

I already mentioned Richard Bann. Richard was a very sweet guy, but you had to get to know him before he'd open up to you. He was a movie connoisseur, and he wrote all of Hef's movie notes for the Friday night movies. Richard used to be a cowboy, so he loved all things related to that. He was very set in a consistent routine, just like Hef was. You would always see him at the same places, at the same times, week after week.

There was also Joel and Alison. As I mentioned, Alison was very dear to Hef. He gave her away at her wedding. She was a social secretary of his in the 70s, and, for many years, she had been a guest at the Mansion. Hef always played backgammon with Joel on Sunday, so you would see this couple at the Mansion almost every day. As I said before, they were like the official welcoming committee, and you could never imagine them being mean or rude to anyone.

Other regulars included another social secretary from the day named Cis Rundle, Playmate Ava Fabian, and a few young girls who would be in and out. There was also a younger movie expert named Jeremy Arnold. Jeremy was the youngest man to be inducted into Hef's movie endeavors, and he knew it was something to be thankful for.

For a very long time, the only young girls who came around Friday and Saturday movie nights regularly, aside from myself, were Alicia and a girl named Jan Klink. But, eventually, Jan grew out of favor, and Alicia would go through spurts where she stopped going, as did I. The new Playmates campaigning for the title of Playmate of the Year would come around, consistently, at the end of each year to be seen so they had a better chance of being chosen for the position (or so they thought they did), but once PMOY was announced, a lot of these girls would filter themselves out and stop coming. That wasn't the case for everyone, but it was true a lot of the time. Most movie regulars were not Playmates for that reason. Occasionally, however, Playmates would stop by to visit.

The FITS girls were a completely different sect of people. They were, generally, girls that would just come up for the pool parties on Sundays, and a lot of them were not really familiar faces. They would be in and out pretty fast. Some of them were very consistent, but, it was sad to say, a lot of people didn't get to know them and treated them as if they were on a lower level. They didn't tend to seem important to people. There were a few FITS girls who would come often enough for the regulars to get to know them, it just wasn't a luxury that was given to all of them. I, having snuck my way in on Fridays, avoided that awkward level. I came in as a regular, having been seen by everyone on Friday and Saturday nights. Everyone knew me. I could come to FITS whenever I liked, but I preferred Friday movies overall. A lot of the politics and hierarchy I didn't even notice until much later, as I submerged myself into this lifestyle. I should have stopped, at this point, and asked myself, "Are you ready for this journey?" But I did not ask. I just jumped right in.

# Fun in the Sun

Shortly after my first visit to the Mansion, I made my way out for a FITS Sunday. It was a very surreal experience. Basically, FITS happened every Sunday. It was the same set up as Friday and Saturday movie nights with the dinner and the movies, but the movie was always a new release that just came into theatres. The other difference was, the four hours before the dinner you could explore the Mansion grounds, and you had the freedom to do whatever you wanted to do (within reason). So, it was an all-day event from 1pm – 9pm. Generally, during these days, Hef played backgammon with Joel while all of the girls would sit around and relax. In the summertime, FITS would take place by the pool. It became a giant pool party. Hef and Joel would sit at a glass table at the far end of the pool, and the girlfriends would be lounging nearby on lawn chairs. Hef would be out until about 3:45pm, at which time he would have all the girls come over for a photo with him. Then, he would head upstairs until dinner. Whenever the weather wasn't ideal, FITS would take place in the game house. On days where Hef wasn't feeling his best, FITS would take place in the library. When I first started coming, this was an extremely rare occurrence. By the end of my time at the Mansion, when Hef was getting older, it always took place in the library. On this particular day, it was occurring in the game house;

however, because Hef and Crystal were getting ready to head to England, he wasn't outside. It was just a few of us girls hanging around the game house together.

Because Hef wasn't there and I didn't know too many of the girls, I took advantage of being able to explore the Mansion grounds for the first time, and I wandered around everywhere. Our day started out at the game house. The game house had a nice, fenced-in patio area where the girls could enjoy an open bar and a nice little snack buffet. When you walked inside the game house, you went through several rooms where the floors were just cushy beds with pillows. These rooms led into the actual game room. In the game room, you could find Pac Man, Playboy Pinball Machines, Donkey Kong, Frogger, a pool table, a foosball table, and many other console and tabletop games. I went into the game house, explored, and played Pac Man. You could also order lunch off of a special menu. The little home-made pizzas they had available to order were always great. That was my food of choice on this particular day.

After eating, one of the girls I was with wanted to go to the pool, so the three of us walked across the Mansion grounds to get to the backyard. By exiting the game house and walking on the stone paths, you could discover the tennis courts, the guest house, and a replica of Hef's star from the Walk of Fame all in front of the house, separated by greenery. The bushes were so dense out there that it was like a forest. Once it cleared, there was a field in front of the house where you could find a wishing well.

As you approach the house from the field, you could clearly see the circular driveway, the fountain, and so many beautiful flowers that ran up the side of the Mansion. When you got to the left side of the house where the paths continued, you could see the famous, picturesque lion statues on top of a very large, towering hill. Once you passed the statues, if you veered off to the right, you'd see the giant lawn (in the summer they would put a volleyball court here), the trampoline, the pool and grotto areas, and the outdoor bathrooms and showers that led to the gym. If you went forward instead of turning right, you'd wind up at the zoo.

Of course, I had to stop to check out the zoo! First, there were tons of birds that just wandered around or sat up on perches. Flamingos, peacocks, and African cranes casually strolled around on the grounds. There were parrots, cockatoos, and more birds that sat on perches and hung from the trees of the zoo. Further down the path, you'd see bunnies in a cage, little squirrel monkeys in a giant habitat, and some larger apes, as well. Coco was always there. Coco was a spider monkey, and she was very sweet. If you went over to her cage, she'd lean up on the side and hang down next to you. She'd point to her side, which told you where she wanted to be scratched. I remembered Coco from *The Girls Next Door,* so I was excited to meet her and spend some time with her.

From there, I crossed the open field and continued on to the pool. The pool was sculpted into a beautiful area made of rocks and bushes. There was a big mountain-like cluster of rocks in the center of the pool, which was hollow inside. If you walked around the pool inside that hollow, it became "the grotto," an indoor hot tub big enough for at least 30 people. It was, by definition, a grotto. I was intrigued, so while the other two girls were lounging around by the pool, I walked into the grotto, sat inside, and surveyed the area of the pool. In fact, for fifteen minutes, I sat with my feet in the warm water. I tuned out all negativity as I focused on the splashing water coming from the waterfall just outside of a hole in a nearby rock. This place was so infamous. How could I not soak in its glory? When I was done, I stood up, forgetting that the grotto had lower walls and ceilings, and I hit my head very hard on a poorly-placed rock. I bounced back down with a jolt of force, and I'm sure the security guard watching the cameras got a good laugh at that. Luckily, I was fine. I watched my head more carefully the second time I stood up, and I slowly exited the man-made cave.

After lounging by the pool for an hour, we journeyed into the bath house. The bath house was built like a large, wooden cabin that stretched back for what seemed like miles. Parts of it were built in wood and other parts in stone. There were chamber doors along the big hallway, each leading to a new restroom. Finally, there was a large, mirrored room with a bed-like floor at the end of the hall and a spiral staircase going down at the back of the room. That staircase led you downstairs to the gym. There were weights, treadmills, bikes, and more all down in the gym. You could see enlarged pictures of past Playmates hanging on the walls by each machine. And, of course, there was a tanning room with two tanning beds, as well as a steam room. I didn't know it at the time, but there was a hidden passage behind one of the mirrors in the gym that led from the kitchen. It was something that I explored with great detail later on, but not at this time. While the other two girls that I was with tanned, I went back up and hung out in the game room.

Once 5pm rolled around, it was movie night. There was a dinner buffet and a movie, like always. However, I do have to say that Sunday was the worst night to experience the movie in my opinion. Because of FITS and the release of a new movie, there were more girls, so cushions were harder to come by. You had to go inside the movie room earlier than normal or you'd have to fight girls for the cushion seats set up front. So, Fridays were better, in that respect. The fear of watching older movies scared off many FITS girls from ever coming on a Friday or Saturday. From that point on, when I went on Sundays I rarely stayed for the movie.

# Hef's Breakup

Near the beginning of my time at the Mansion, I went on vacation. While I was gone, everything that I knew about the Playboy Mansion changed. Crystal Harris, Hef's finance, left him five days before their wedding. She said she was going out to the drug store and, instead, took off. She was the "runaway bride" in the world of Playboy. Funny enough, because I was away and new to this world, I read about this on the internet. That information shook my world. Everything changed within an instant, and Hef was on the prowl again. Because an issue of Playboy was already created with a photo of Crystal on the cover as "the new Mrs. Hefner," Hef made the last-minute decision to put a "runaway bride" sticker over part of her photo.

I had no idea about this at the time, but I found out one of the major reasons why she left much later. I will get into that later when I begin telling you about my friendship with Crystal.

Because of her disappearance, the rules had changed. Rather than being scared to talk to Hef due to Crystal's wrath, you could now openly talk to him. There was no more reason to be fearful of the all-controlling Crystal. All that anyone had ever told me about her was to fear her and stay away. I won't lie, I was scared of her. I felt a little odd about going back to the Mansion after this, just because I hated change and I wondered how different it would be, but I still continued to go.

After my vacation ended, I didn't go on Friday as I usually did. Instead, I went to another FITS Sunday. This time, it also happened to be on Father's Day, so Hef was out all day long, but he was playing backgammon with his children and Joel. Of course, more girls showed up than usual to throw themselves at him because he was now considered "single." There was a foreign girl that I had never met before (she didn't stick around long) who brought him an actual bunny rabbit as a gift. That was priceless; however, Hef didn't seem interested, at all. When she spoke to him from over his shoulder, he concentrated harder on his backgammon game; he practically shooed her away.

From what I could understand at the time, I thought that Hef had "moved on" from his ex to her best friend Anna. I figured that was inevitable. You could tell when she was around Crystal and Hef that there was something going on there. To be honest, when Hef and Crystal were engaged, Anna was another girlfriend. I found that out later. It was an unspoken thing that was, basically, hidden in the eyes of the public, but she had a room at the Mansion. She lived there, and she followed all the rules that the girlfriends lived by, which included a 9pm daily curfew (and it was earlier most days because she had to attend certain events throughout the week with Hef). It also included a monthly allowance. It was on the down-low since Crystal and Hef got engaged, but Anna had been a girlfriend for quite a while before Crystal left. Crystal leaving gave a reason to make that fact known. That week, someone tweeted Crystal about how horrible it was that her best friend was now dating Hef, and Crystal just replied, "No, Anna's not dating him. She's just staying for me to make sure that Hef finds himself a good girl to take my place." In fact, almost a year later, Anna's mother stated, publically that "Hef and Anna aren't dating. Anna's just a good friend staying with him." I think Anna said that to get people off of her case because she was very much considered a girlfriend. Also, many people publicly attacked her and called her a "home-wrecker" when they found out she was with Hef, so I do not blame her for not being up front about their relationship, at all. She got a lot of unnecessary anger directed at her from Hef and Crystal fans.

Anna was a very quiet and soft-spoken girl when she was at the Mansion, because it seemed that she felt safe that way. However, when she moved out, she came out of her shell with me and was a very spunky and fun person to be around. (We actually became good friends later.) I think she was also Hef's favorite for a long time after Crystal left. You could see the way that Hef looked at her when she spoke, and he absolutely adored her. Because of this, she got away with everything. Her curfews became looser and looser, and she got "days off" that the other girls didn't seem to have.

To top it all off, one night shortly after Crystal left, Shera Bechard, a Playmate that I had seen around but had never known, was whispering to people. She told them that Hef was calling girls in and that she was moving into the Mansion. I could tell that this was true because he started following her on twitter. (A tip about Hef at this point in his life: He only followed his sons, Playboy, and his girlfriends on twitter. If you ever wanted to tell who was truly a girlfriend, you checked his twitter to see who he was following.) So, it seemed that Hef had Anna as one girlfriend, and Shera was moving in as well. Of course, I expected that there would be one more to follow soon.

This first night I was back, though, Anna wasn't there, so Shera took her place on the couch next to Hef, and she went upstairs with him afterwards. But, as I said before, even though Shera actually moved in as the "Number One Girlfriend," Anna seemed to be the favorite. There was a look he gave her that I've never seen him give anyone else.

This same day, the Shannon twins (as seen on the last season of *The Girls Next Door*) were also rumored to be moving back into the Mansion, but this was proven false. Karissa and Kristina Shannon were moving back into the bunny house because their lease ran out. They were not moving back with Hef, and they were not with him. Those two girls were way too wild to abide by Hef's rules. And, because of this, even their move into the Bunny House lasted for an extremely short period of time. They showed up for the movie that Sunday, and I laid right next to one of them on the cushions. In fact, the three of us shared two cushions because they ran out of space, and they asked me to share. We spoke a lot, and they, very openly, came out about how they couldn't deal with the rules that Hef put upon them, so they could never be girlfriends again.

They began to say very nice things to me, and I appreciated it.

"You're so pretty. You should be an actress!!"

"I am an actress!"

"That's great!! You totally can be! I love your freckles. Have you done Playboy?"

"No."

"Oh, that's great. A lot of television shows won't take you seriously once you've done the magazine, but you would make a GREAT Playmate!"

"Awww. Thank you!"

They were very sweet, and I wanted them to stick around. Unfortunately, those girls only stayed at the Bunny House for an extremely short period of time. They moved on faster than anyone, and, as I said, it was very easy to see why.

# Goodbye, Russell

Despite the fact that I was on a high from being allowed at the Mansion on the weekends whenever I pleased, I tried not to cut all ties with Russell and Vanessa right away because I didn't want them to feel hurt or like I was just shutting them out because I got to the Playboy Mansion. I knew they were horrible people, but I still didn't want to hurt anyone's feelings. Plus, I felt some sort of obligation to be nice to them. I hated going out with them, but, at the time of this event, I was so glad that Kristina had just come back into town, and I wanted to see her again. In fact, I probably wouldn't have mustered up the motivation to actually make it to Russell's if she had not come back. I had attended the Mansion movie night before heading out, and I was on top of the world. Who cared what Russell thought? I was one of Hef's guests.

As I arrived at Russell's, he gave me a nasty look, "You're wearing that?"

"Yeah. I wore it to the Mansion, too. Hef seemed to be okay with it." I really wanted to toy with Russell for saying such a horrible thing to me. Too many girls let him talk to them that way. I wasn't about to. He just glared at me and went on his way.

There was an issue, on this particular night, where a friend of Russell's brought two "husky" girls to the club with us. All of Russell's girls tore them to pieces. It was disgusting how they treated these poor girls. One of the big girls got drunk before we even left Russell's house. Kristina, Melina, and I, the tenured girls, were all upstairs with Russell and Vanessa, while all the new girls were downstairs. We went down, and this big, drunk girl had busted her dress open. She was hysterically crying. Vanessa went to her closet to find a dress for her, but this poor girl had to squeeze into it with all of her might. Kristina, specifically, hated these girls because they were bigger. She looked at me with disgust, "Vanessa can never wear that dress again. What was she thinking?" I heard it all night.

"Did you see the bouncers when the fat girls got out of the limo? They rolled their eyes. They cannot be seen out with girls like me and you."

"That girl is so gross. Why is she here?"

I truly felt bad. They didn't ask to be treated like this, and it wasn't fair to them. This just stacked onto the reasons why Russell and his crew were so horrible. This incident, specifically, changed my opinion of Kristina a lot, too. She was the only one that I liked, and her judgmental attitude was getting to me. Before, when she disliked people, at least there was a valid reason behind it. Now, she was just being mean.

As we rode back to Russell's in the limo, my mind wandered. I was on the top of Russell's group, yes, but being on top of a pile of crap is still sitting on a pile of crap. Russell meant nothing to me. At the Mansion, people treated me well, which was something Russell didn't do to anyone. Seeing how nice everyone was at the Mansion versus how cruel Russell was truly opened my eyes that I was on the right path. It was ironic that Russell was the epitome of what people thought happened at the Mansion: crazy sex and drugs. In reality, that didn't exist in that world anymore. The Mansion was a center of peace and quiet (unless there was a party going on). Russell was a ball of chaos.

I was finally able to accept how I felt about Russell and Vanessa without being kind about it once I stepped back and looked at what was happening from a distance. Clearly, I hung out with Russell because he was a contact. I hated going out with Russell and Vanessa. We wound up lost in random places and abandoned by the limo. Although they did not do this to me, I watched them use peer pressure to try and get girls to have sex with them and to do drugs or "you'll never work again." It just wasn't fun for me. I'm not that person. Not only did I not sleep around nor did I do drugs, but I didn't even drink! I hung around them because I thought Russell could help me with my career. When I realized that wasn't true, I stuck around for no reason other than the fact that I felt a false sense of obligation. My contact into the Mansion was a girl I met through him, but that was a complete coincidence. He didn't know her involvement at the Mansion and had nothing to do with me getting there except bringing her to an event with me. I had to separate myself from the negativity that was Russell.

Well, when I started going to the Mansion each week, I found a job as a brand ambassador that paid more and had better hours than my job at Victoria's Secret. That, mixed with the mean people I had to deal with on a daily basis in Los Angeles, was motivation for me to leave Victoria's Secret. This new job was a fun marketing job that worked me from early in the morning until about 9pm on Fridays, Saturdays, and Sundays. Luckily, I was able to leave early from work on Fridays to make it to movie nights. (Though I couldn't attend FITS while I was working this job, which is another reason why I never really went to FITS during my first year at the Mansion. But, it was great because it left my whole week open for auditions, filming, and anything else that I needed to accomplish.)

Needless to say, my weekends were swamped at this point, and it exhausted me. I went from seeing Russell and Vanessa once a week to once a month because of how demanding my work was on the weekends (and they almost never went out during the week at this time). Plus, on Fridays, I spent my evenings at the Playboy Mansion. I enjoyed the Mansion, and I enjoyed being around Hef so much that I couldn't bear to be around the miserable, shallow lives of Vanessa and Russell. My friends at the Mansion were, generally, nice. Russell and Vanessa were not. In fact, they weren't even friends. Friends do not objectify each other. Russell used us to make him look good, and friends shouldn't do that. Friends let you talk to people while you're out with them. Friends let you bring your boyfriend if you want. Friends let you dress how you want and not the way that will make them look the best. Russell did all this and more. You had to dress to his approval; you couldn't talk to anyone else but him; you couldn't leave for too long to go to the bathroom. That's not a friend.

After a couple of months at the Mansion, I found out from Kristina that Russell's crew was furious with me. They were offended that I cut their time to go to the Mansion.  I didn't want to be on bad terms with them, even if they weren't my favorite people, so...back into the slavery of Russell I went. My life was back to being around the drama. It's a character flaw of mine that I never want anyone to be upset with me, so I did want to try and keep Russell and Vanessa from being angry. That being said, I made an attempt to go out with Russell a bit after that. We all had dinner at Pink Taco one Tuesday, and then I went out with them that Friday. Everything seemed to fit back into place. He, of course, spent the whole time asking me crude questions.

"Do you have sex with Hef? Does he lick your boobies? What's he like? Does he like you?"

I was horribly offended. He knew that I was engaged, and I was not like that. The Mansion was not like that. I finally snapped.

I decided that I did not need that from him! From that point on, I cut my ties with Russell. He had no respect for anyone, and I was done dealing with it. We didn't exactly have a true falling out, because that's not the person I am, but we definitely didn't speak anymore. I stopped going out with them altogether, and I, slowly but surely, got less and less invites to go out with them at all. I saw them a few times at the Kandy parties at the Mansion, and there was always this sick feeling of joy in my mind when they saw me in Hef's cabana or roped off in Hef's section where they couldn't go. That man once looked at me like I was his property. For him to see what used to be his "prisoner" hanging with the person that he more or less aspired to be like was revenge enough. (Though Hef is respectful and kind, and Russell would never be like him as hard as he tried.)

I never went out of my way to bad-mouth Russell, but when people asked me about him, I was always honest on my thoughts and feelings about him. True, it was nice that they didn't force me to do anything I didn't want to do, but the peer pressure to others and horrible attitude was enough to drive anyone crazy. Kristina approached me once I began to disappear from their lives. She said that they thought I left them for the Playboy Mansion, so I must have thought I was better than them. This was my reply: "Where I go and who I hang out with does not define me. I do not think I am better than you because I hang out at the Playboy Mansion. I enjoy my time there. I never enjoyed my time with Russell. Where I am now I have true friends who treat me well. That was something that Russell could never give me. I have not changed as a person. I always just floated behind Russell and you girls watching the horror you inflict. I had no place being with you, as I felt guilty about the pain you inflicted on others. I am just finally doing what I enjoy doing. I am no longer following someone who is lost."

Thus ended my thoughts, feelings, and journeys with Russell on any personal level. I was ashamed to have ever been seen hanging around him, but it put me where I needed to be on my path to move forward. I was very blessed that, through all the trials and tribulations with them, I never changed. I knew who I was. I never compromised myself for them in any way like many of their followers did.

And, through it all, Russell did teach me a few lessons. He taught me not to always trust everyone in this industry. He taught me to always be on my guard whenever I went out. I learned how to keep myself safe. Because of him, I was less naïve and more aware of my surroundings, which, I guess, can only be a good thing. I learned the lessons that I needed to survive in this town.

True, I was sad to have lost Kristina by leaving the group, but, if she was going to stick by Russell's side, then she wasn't a true friend. There would be many more friends to come in my future at the Mansion. After all, I was so neutral that I became everyone's best friend, it seemed.

# The Truth Behind Crystal Leaving

The movie night that took place on Friday, June 25th, 2011 was an eye-opening experience for me. It was the first time I actually saw Hef happy and interactive with everyone. To be honest, Crystal left Hef on the day her music album released, so I didn't know if it was just her trying to get publicity because of that or if it was a plan between Hef and Crystal. Maybe that was planned on both of their parts? I didn't know how Hollywood was, and I wasn't going to believe anything about it either way until I had proof. In my mind, it was plausible for Crystal's leaving to be set up by anyone and everyone, and I was very curious about it. Luckily for me, all my questions were answered on this evening.

On this particular night, Hef came down, sat in his seat, and waved to each girl at the table, which he never did before. He waved at the Playmates and then to me. He looked each one of us in the eyes and smiled. He even blew kisses at us. He then began to talk to his good friend Ray Anthony (and then turned to all of us who were around) about the incident with Crystal. He confided to us that she really surprised him. He said that he was very upset by it, and he even called her a monster. After a pause, he added, "I can't be mad at her. She did me a favor. She ended it early. Can you imagine how horrible it would have been if she decided to do this after we were married? It's better that she did it now. I can, at least, appreciate that." He also added that he felt their relationship suffering and getting weird in the last couple of weeks. He ended by telling us that he should have known it was coming.

Later, one of the butlers added that he heard that they had fought over a prenuptial agreement, and that she was planning on breaking up with him at the altar, but no one would buy her interview for enough money. That part was, of course, a rumor that I didn't know the validity of. But the words that came out of Hef's mouth were solid gold for me. That was how he truly felt about the situation. At this moment, I knew that the media was correct. Crystal left Hef, and Hef was clueless about the situation until it happened.

After dinner, the movie playing was *Mr. Smith Goes to Washington*. I had seen it before in high school, and I was not excited to watch it again because I knew how long it was. We started off with me, another girl, and the twins down on the floor on the cushions at the beginning of the movie. The twins piled out almost immediately. Then, the other girl left. By the end of the flick, all the guests wound up hanging out in the dining room except about three or four of us. When the movie ended, Hef stayed very actively engaged with everyone. Again, this was new. I don't know if it was because he didn't have a girlfriend around or if he was just in a good mood because Crystal was gone. He looked at each of us and asked where all the guys were this evening. It was true, most of his older friends didn't turn out this week. He said, "Don't get me wrong, I love being surrounded by beautiful women." He laughed some, walked by us, and said, "Goodnight ladies. Thank you for coming out," and headed upstairs. It was the most talkative and happy I had seen him at this point. I learned that he was always very engaging after the movies ended in that brief time before he went upstairs for his 9pm bedtime. (Now, I don't know if he went to sleep at 9, but he was upstairs for good each night as soon as the movie was over.)

That evening, he announced on his twitter that Shera, the girl who moved in, was officially his new girlfriend. He then added that Anna was really just his best friend. I could actually believe that at that time. But, again, this proved to be false. He slowly allowed people to see that she was a girlfriend as time went on to transition smoothly into that. That way, no one asked questions. Plus, Shera would tweet for him, and Anna, I'm sure, was in her ear asking her not to announce her as a girlfriend for her own sake. A while later, he announced that she was and always had been a girlfriend. So, now that that was cleared up, Hef was dating Anna and Shera, and there was room for one more girl now that there were rumors that if his special about the runaway bride went well, he'd do another season of *The Girls Next Door*! (This never actually happened, but it was a rumor at the time.)

Thinking about it, I was relieved to have Crystal gone because, as I said before, I was taught from my first day to be afraid of her. Shera seemed like a nicer person, and the whole dynamic changed with her there. Shera Bechard, Hef's new number-one girlfriend, was a pretty, classy Canadian woman. Through movie nights (and, especially, the July 4th party), I began speaking with her. My first impression of her was that she was a kind person who wanted to start several Playmate charities, especially charities involving animals. I definitely liked Shera, though, I know a lot of people who didn't. I thought she was best for Hef in his time of need.

Looking back on it, because she wasn't as protective as Crystal, the Mansion became a bit of a party house while Shera was there. Girls that Crystal wanted nothing to do with would come up and stay for extended periods of time to visit for the parties. They weren't afraid of Shera, so they would do whatever they wanted without the fear of being kicked out. They would take advantage of the staff and ability to be around now that Crystal, their number one enemy, was gone. So, during this part of our story (and for my next year at the Mansion), the environment was more or less in a constant state of partying.

# The Party Crowd

Everyone who knows anything about Playboy knows that the Playboy Mansion parties hosted by Hef were, at one point, potentially the best in the world. They were unbeatable. Sure, they've gotten a little less eccentric over the years, but they are definitely still worth attending. The parties have changed a lot since the 90s and even since the early 2000s. At this point at the Mansion, there were three main types of parties. There were random parties by different companies who chose to buy out the Mansion for a night, there were Hef's parties, and there were "Karma" parties (also known as Kandy parties).

The random parties hosted by companies who bought out the Mansion for the night took place outside. The guests for those events were never allowed inside the Mansion, and Hef almost never came out for those, except maybe to take a photo or two and go right back upstairs. Hef's guests could technically never go to those events, as they were not invited to them. They were private events. There were many occasions where I was inside the Mansion after a movie night and they had a security guard standing by the back patio to ensure that the people inside the Mansion didn't make it out back into those events and vice versa.

Hef's parties were the infamous parties that everyone had heard of. They were the best of the best. Throughout my stay at the Mansion, Hef hosted the following parties: July 4th, *The Midsummer Night's Dream* Party, and the New Year's Party. There were also smaller get-together events for regulars and friends, such as the Easter Celebration, the Superbowl party, and *Casablanca* Night. Hef would always make an appearance at his own parties; however, as he got older, those appearances became shorter and shorter. (Near the end of my time, he barely came out for 30 minutes at his own party.)

The Karma/Kandy parties were awful. They were just not my cup of tea. They were hosted by an organization of guys who sold tickets to anyone with money looking to come up and party for a night. Any rich pervert with $1,000 could pay to attend the party. Any rich pervert with $10,000 to spare could have his own cabana. That was always the worst approach—having someone buy their way up to the Mansion for a night. They thought that they owned any of the girls they saw there because they paid money to be there. Let me tell you, that is not the case, and anyone who thinks that way is slime. There was great food and décor at these events, but it was just a bunch of random people partying and paying a fortune for a chance to see the Mansion. These parties consisted of Kandy Masquerade, Kandyland, and Kandy Halloween. The Halloween party was the only one I ever cared about or attended. I didn't care about the others because Karma parties were always over-crowded and overdone. I dealt with the Halloween party because I loved Halloween. By the end of my time at the Mansion, the Karma Foundation was more or less booted from there, and the Kandy parties took place at other locations. I heard that they had some type of falling out with Playboy that I don't know the details of, and that was okay by me.

For the most part, I didn't like attending any parties. I'm a homebody, so I would much rather hang out at home than go out and party. But, my attendance at the events was necessary if I wanted to stay in good with everyone. Everyone told me that the Mansion office would look down on me if I decided not to attend too many parties in a row, and I'd even potentially stop getting invited to the movie nights that I loved. That being said, I went because I felt that I had to out of obligation. I wanted to keep attending movie nights, so the parties were a must. The following parties were the ones you could find me at, in the order that I first attended them:

## July 4th

Hef's July 4th parties were definitely some of my favorite parties. They consisted of a smaller amount of guests and a larger amount of food. Plus, it was a daytime event, so it was more like a barbeque than a party, which is why I loved it so much. On July 4th, the backyard of the Mansion grounds became flooded with burger stands, hotdog stands, popcorn carts, ice cream stations, popsicles, and more. The first time I went to one of these parties, I was shocked to see a giant, inflatable slip n' slide that fell down the side lawn towards the gate entrance. There were two tracks so that girls could race each other down it. It was inflatable, yes, but it was also dangerous. The first two years that I attended the event, no one got majorly hurt. A lot of us got wounds from it, but they were small. I got a cut and burn on my right elbow and a few other girls got burns on their butts. It was worth it, though. A lot of girls were afraid to try it out because of the steep drop. (You can see what I'm talking about in the later seasons of *The Girls Next Door*.) The third year I was there, one of the Playmates really hurt herself on it, so in the following years, we were required to sign waivers before going down it. They also started a rule making sure no one could go down it head first, but my husband came to several events with Marston Hefner later on, so I watched the butlers look the other way when the guys went down head first. They weren't happy about it, but Marston lived there, so they couldn't do anything about it.

Aside from the amazing amounts of all-American food and the fun races down the slip n' slide, you could choose to play volleyball, sunbathe by the pool, swim in the pool on the dozens of fun floats, or relax in the grotto. In the later years, the guys also set up beer pong to play by the pool.

The first year that I went to the July 4th party, we sat around, swam, and had a lot of fun. Hef came out and took photos with all of the girls by the giant slide. One of these photos with me in it was actually put up on his photo hallway upstairs at the Mansion for a bit. It was great to know that a photo of me with Hef and the girls was hanging up at the Playboy Mansion for a little while.

Now, on this particular Independence Day (the first time I went), it was flooded with ladies because Crystal had just left. There was no particular area that separated Hef from the rest of the guests, so many girls were running around and taking photos with him. There were tremendous amounts of group photos circling around from that party because of all of the women that attended. Shera didn't mind, though. She wasn't jealous like that. That particular July 4th was the first time that I got to bond with Shera. I also met Trisha Frick that day. Little did I know, Trisha would become one of my best friends for the next year.

Trisha Frick was a very cute girl from Texas. She was a true girl-next-door type who seemed very out-of-place at the Mansion. She was actually staying with Hef at this time, and continued to stay with him throughout the end of the summer. I asked Trisha how she started coming to the Mansion. Trisha had written Hef a letter about how much she admired him. In the letter, she said that if she could come visit, it would make her life. Hef replied and invited Trisha to the Mansion for a visit. From that point on, she came to spend a month in the house every year or so. On this July 4th, she was back staying at the Mansion. She was a very sweet girl. She did not fit in in the world of Playboy, but I really enjoyed that about her, because I didn't really fit in either. Because of that, we got along well.

The same year that Trisha was visiting, several girls from different places flew in to spend a week at the Mansion. Crystal would never have allowed them to come and stay upstairs in the house, but Crystal was no longer around, and they took advantage of that. They were pretty much users, and, while Crystal was gone, this gaggle of girls was always around the week surrounding every major party. I didn't really get to know any of them because they were pretty stuck up and formed their own group.

Each year after that, the July 4th parties never let me down... more or less. The great All-American fun never stopped blowing me away, and the epic slip n' slide never disappeared. I almost have nothing but great memories about every July 4th party that I went to.

I did have one bad repercussion from the event in 2014. Because my husband and I came to the event with Marston this year, I got in trouble. Because I was on Hef's list and I didn't check in at the parking deck and take a shuttle in, I got a stern email. Despite the fact that I was with Marston, I did not follow the correct "sign-in" protocol, and following the rules is always a must at the Mansion. It was alright, though, as I didn't get in too much trouble from it. I just received a warning email that I needed to correct my mistake, and I never made that mistake again. It wasn't enough of an issue to ruin my Independence Day fun. The July 4th parties always have a happy place in my mind.

## A Midsummer Night's Dream

In the August of my first year at the Mansion, two incredible things happened on the same day. One, I was notified that I had been permanently added to the movie night guest list. This meant that I could come up on any Friday or Saturday movie night without having to ask first. It also meant that I could attend any FITS I wanted without having to ask as well. Two, I got my personal invite from Hef to *the Midsummer Night's Dream* Party. *The Midsummer Night's Dream* or "Midsummers" (as we called it) was Hef's most famous party, and it tended to be everyone's favorite. It was mystical, sexy, and incredibly fun. I got an email in my inbox from "HEF." I clicked on it, and it read, "HEF has sent you an invitation." Once I clicked on that, the official invite to Midsummers came up with a beautiful, painted pinup image from Olivia, Playboy's animation artist. It was stunning, and I was so excited. This was the only invite that I ever received that came in this way, actually.

In preparation, I had to make sure that I looked perfect for the party. I had to find a corset because, from what I had seen, all the bunnies and girlfriends wore a corset there (which definitely wasn't true as far as my friends went, but this was the impression that I was under for my first event.) I'd never owned a corset, so I was excited to find the perfect one. It was rich blue, and it tied up the back. It had blue boy shorts, and I got a white bra for under it and white lace for my hair.

My first impression of Midsummers was that it was more of a large, industry-networking event than a crazy party. There were a lot of people there looking to hand out business cards. Well, I met up with Alicia, the girl who originally got me into the Mansion, at the beginning of the night. This was actually the first time I was with Alicia at the Mansion, so this was a new experience for me in that regard. We met up at the garage and were driven to the Mansion on a shuttle together with her friend and Morgan, Hef's nephew. (At this point, from what she had said, Alicia was sleeping with Morgan, but it wasn't very serious.)

The theme for the party this year was Arabian Nights, so when we arrived, there were camels relaxing off in the grass by the wishing well. We took pictures with the camels, walked by all the painted girls, and then went into the tents outside. The whole backyard was tented, and you couldn't even tell it was the same place I went to every week. There were tents interwoven together and there was a stage to the left. There were TV's everywhere playing footage of past events and a buffet off to the right by the pool houses. The entire area was draped in pinks and blues, and there were genie pillows around small tables to sit on and eat at. I really wanted to say "Hi" to Hef, but he was with all of his bodyguards and girls off at a private tent. You couldn't even get near the tent. I did get to say "Hi" to Shera and her sister for a second, though. That was nice, at least. I spent the night running around with Alicia, but she was a little too much for me. I think she believed that because she got me into the Mansion in the first place, that I had to stay with her as her guest for the entire night, but since I had been coming without her for some time, I knew people that she didn't. When I'd go off to say "Hi" to someone without her, she'd look around for me and then call me...as if I was committing a crime. She ran around and socialized with what seemed like everyone there. She did it so quickly I couldn't keep up. I was able to break away a few times to get food or chat with someone that I knew, but whenever I was gone too long, I got the call from Alicia.

I left the event early because I had to work the next day. What an interesting night. The party aspect was boring for me, but the experience was enticing.

After Midsummers that first year, Trisha had to leave for Texas. Her stay at the Mansion had come to an end. I was saddened by this, as I did like Trisha a lot. We said our goodbyes one Sunday afternoon, and she was off. The next week, I went back for a movie and Trisha was back! She told me that she had left, and the next day Hef had called her and asked her to move in. She had moved back within days. I was excited to have her around all the time, and she would be at all of my first Playboy Mansion events with me. She was with me at the next Midsummers that I attended as well. Each year, Midsummers seemed to get better and better, and I was happy to have someone I could relate to going through the Playboy Mansion experiences with me.

## Kandy Halloween

As I mentioned before, the Kandy events were not my favorite parties. They were over-crowded, as Karma sold tickets to anyone wanting to come up and party at the Mansion for a night. As regulars of Hef's, the first year I went we were allowed to come up early before the party to attend our regularly-scheduled movie night. So, I pulled up to my first Kandy Halloween in October of 2011, as I did for any normal movie night. This time, however, I was in costume.

Unfortunately, there was an issue of me getting in for the movie night. The security guard at the intercom told me to go away because I was not on the list. He was very insistent and very rude. I, immediately, called Hef's secretary to find out that the guy was looking at the wrong list. She resolved it, and I got in. He was rude, but it was a mistake. They were stressed, and I had to get over it, but it was hard for me to shake off that issue at first. I went to dinner, and during the movie, I went with the girls to the guest house to get ready. We goofed off, fixed up our makeup, and the girls who were not in costume got into their costumes. Then we went back, took pictures, and waited for the movie to get out so we could enter the party with Hef.

Once the movie finished, Hef came strolling out into the Great Hall. He gathered up all of us regulars, and security gave us our wrist bands that were a special color, indicating that we were allowed to enter the Mansion whenever we wanted. (No one else could come inside because it wasn't Hef's party and the inside was considered private property. So, throughout the night, I was allowed back and forth inside and out, unlike anyone else who was there.) At this point, we followed Hef and security to the haunted maze. We cut the line for the haunted house, following Hef, his girlfriends, and the Playmates right into the funhouse. I have to say, watching Hef in that maze, you couldn't tell his age at all. He was so excited by all the horrific scenes. He would laugh when things jumped out, and he went right up to the monsters to get a closer look. They were a little taken aback to find Hugh Hefner coming right up to their faces. Following our exit from the tented maze, we made our way to Hef's cabana. That was a highlight for me, to be taken through a crowd with Hef and security, being sent through the haunted maze with Hef, and getting to cut the extremely long line for the haunted house. The best part was that Russell happened to be there and just so happened to see me go through the crowd with Hef. I smiled and waved at him and Vanessa to be sure they saw me. That may have been a little mean, but Russell deserved that.

Once we arrived at Hef's cabana, we were ushered around the cushions circling Hef. The butlers took our drink orders, and we watched as everyone at the party stared at us. Since it was a party that people bought their way into through Karma, barely anyone there knew Hef on any personal level, nor had they seen him before. So, everyone in the crowd was snapping photos of us, leaning up to the sides of the gates of the cabana like animals trying to get a glimpse of Hef.

But, as expected for a Karma party, I left early due to the enormous crowd. There was too much hustle and bustle for me...too many guys scheming to get with all the scantily clad women that paid their way up for the night. Unfortunately, that night there was a lot of negativity and shallowness as well. This was the first night I saw a separation between Playmates and non-Playmates. Some of the Playmates that were there were offended that some of the girls in the cabana were not Playmates, despite the fact they were invited in. It was silly, but some of the girls had a superiority complex. It was something that I saw a lot in the future, but I was able to look past it, as most girls were nice to me. I worked with a lot of the Playmates for Bench Warmer Trading Cards in the future, so we were, generally, all friends and there was no judgment.

Because this year was the year where Shera was reigning as number-one girlfriend, the crowd of girls that would stay at the Mansion just for the parties was there for the event. There were 12 girls staying at the Mansion, most of which Crystal would never have approved of being on her turf. Hef's entourage had grown in a matter of minutes without Crystal around.

The Halloween parties, in the years to come, evolved into more of a Playboy affair. They began combining the Karma Party with Hef's party, and, inevitably, the Halloween Party became Playboy's affair once more. They were always fun despite the large crowds. One year, my man and I went with Marston, and we had a great time. They were the best parties to go to because of the Haunted Houses, so, to this day, I still look back on them fondly.


## New Year's Eve

The New Year's party was unlike any other event at the Mansion. Rather than being flooded with people, it was a small, elegant, affair. Despite the excitement of the New Year, it stayed relatively quiet. We dressed in elegant attire, sat at tables to eat seafood meals, and waited for the ball to drop. The invitation requested the dress code be "black tie or lingerie." I didn't want to dress out of place (nor did I particularly care to dress in lingerie), so I texted a friend that had been to the event before. She told me that only the new girls dress in lingerie, and they always looked out of place. She said, "Everyone comes in nice gowns." So, I joined the occasion and went in a nice, silver dress. It wound up that, for several years, my signature move for New Year's parties was to wear different silver dresses. Of course, during the years that he wasn't there, I left early to see my man at midnight so we could kiss.

At my first New Year's party, I left the event at 11:15pm and made it back at home at 11:55pm to see the ball drop, but there was nowhere to park in my neighborhood due to all the celebrations. I had to park a neighborhood away, run the couple of blocks it took me to get home in big, gaudy heels, and fiddle with the door at top speed to make it inside my apartment. I felt like Cinderella running out of the party just before midnight. I made it back just in time. Unfortunately, Damian had to pick up our friend from the airport and had stepped out briefly. So, I picked up my cat and kissed him on the lips at midnight as I rushed in. The first ten minutes of 2012 I spent cuddling with my cat, and I knew that would usher in a good year. (And what a great year it turned out to be.)

To sum up, the New Year's Eve parties were always nice and quiet. I don't have too many interesting stories from those events because they were just fun and slightly bland. For several years, I only spent a few hours at each of these parties, and the other couple of years, I spent hanging out with Damian and Marston. They were the blander, plain Mansion parties. But, of course, they were still fun.

## Casablanca Night

After the beginning of a new year, the parties went on hold for a while. The first big party-like event that occurred after the beginning of the year was *Casablanca* Night, which happened in early April. Because Hef stopped having big birthday parties, the only way he really celebrated his birthday with friends and family at this point was on *Casablanca* Night. It came once a year on the Friday before Hef's birthday (while I was there). It was a celebration where all the movie night regulars dressed up in 1940s/50s attire (with the women in dresses and the men in white suits) and had a nice lobster dinner. Then, we all went into to the movie room to watch *Casablanca*, Hef's favorite movie. After the movie, the dining room of the Mansion was turned into "Rick's Café Americano" where caviar and champagne were served. I had never had caviar until my first *Casablanca* experience, and I wasn't disappointed. They taught me that caviar was best when treated like salt. If you put a little (not a lot) on top of a cracker with egg and chives, it tasted great.

Now, seeing as how it was a celebration of Hef's birthday, this first year I decided that I had to make him a nice present. But what do you get for the man who has it all? I knew that he liked hand-made gifts the best, but what to make?

I decided on a painting. I made a painting of Hef as Sherlock Holmes (because he loves Sherlock Holmes) and presented it to him that night. He saw it, got very excited, and showed it around to all of his friends. Later on, Trisha sent me a photo of it hanging upstairs. My painting was hanging up at the Playboy Mansion. How many people can say that? I had a picture on Hef's photo wall, and I had a painting at the Playboy Mansion. I was on top of the world.

When asked about *Casablanca* night on Twitter, Hef said, "The Casablanca Night screening is attended by close friends and centerfolds, Joe. Sharing "Casablanca" with close friends, topped by champagne & caviar by candlelight, made for a perfect birthday celebration."

As time went by, I had seen *Casablanca* numerous times. I know the film almost word by word now. But, I have to say, the more you watch it, the better it gets. You begin to catch things that you hadn't caught before, and you appreciate all that is hidden within the script. It was a small celebration of watching a classic movie, and I loved *Casablanca* Night. It was always the same, but so was life in pretty much every aspect of the Playboy Mansion. I was a big fan of routine, as someone with OCD, so I treasured *Casablanca* Night each year.

## Easter

Easter was a wonderful time at the Playboy Mansion, and while I was there, it almost always happened on the same weekend as *Casablanca* night. It was a very small party with Playmates and their families. You would come up, hang by the pool, participate in a huge Easter egg hunt, and get to play in an enormous petting zoo! The first year I was at Easter, Trisha and I collected oranges off of one of the trees at the tennis courts. We turned them in as eggs with the counters for the egg hunt. The workers laughed and actually told us they would count them as eggs.

Each year there were baby bunnies, chicks, ducks, and a lively little joey present. The joey would jump into a sack if you held it in front of him, and then you could hold him. There was always an alligator, a porcupine, snakes, owls, and more. It was a wonderful time to be had for all animal lovers. Not to mention, Easter was a time for celebrities to come out. The first year I got a photo with Gene Simmons from *Kiss*, and the second year I got a photo with Travis Barker from *Blink 182*.

There isn't much else to say about the Easter celebrations because they were very short, only lasting about three hours; however, it was always worth it to go to catch up with everyone you knew and get to play with exotic and adorable animals for a few hours.

## Other Small Events

Aside from the big events that I mentioned above, there were a few other Mansion events that only weekend regulars (and a few others) got invited to that were fun to attend from time to time. Each year in January there was a Super Bowl party where everyone would come together, eat nice food, and enter into a betting pool for the Super Bowl.

We would all meet up to watch the Golden Globes and the Oscars, as well. We would enter into betting pools for the award winners in those, too. Those parties were treated more like larger FITS events. We would eat, hang around, and watch the events on the big screen.

Throughout all of my experiences within my first year at the Mansion, I began to get much closer to Trisha. During the time Trisha went through her journey of moving into the Mansion and spending time living with Hef, I was beside her. As we closed into the spring of 2012, Trisha and I were about to see some big changes coming our way, and they were definitely interesting.

# The Cool Crowd

Aside from how Trisha Frick came to live at the Mansion, there's so much more to say about her. To this day, I miss her a lot, as we were friends for quite some time. For the majority of her stay at the Mansion, she wasn't referred to as a girlfriend, rather a "friend" who stayed at the Mansion. For a long time, it was Shera and Anna as "girlfriends" and Trisha was a "visiting friend," according to Hef. At random, over the spring of 2012, Trisha was finally announced to be Hef's girlfriend. Her relationship with him never really changed, but he finally publicly announced her as a girlfriend on twitter. We joked with her about the situation a bit, saying, "Congrats on finally be[ing] upgraded!"

Trisha was the sweetest girl, but she wasn't, necessarily, the idea of a Playboy beauty. In fact, we were pretty sure that it was because of her looks that Hef refused to call her a girlfriend for a long time. She lost a lot of weight, toned herself up, and eventually got her lips done. At this point, he called her a girlfriend. She did everything she could for Hef's approval (as well as that of the general populous). I thought she was always beautiful the way she was, and it made me sad to see her try so hard to be accepted when I don't think she needed to.

From what I understood, Trisha's life in Texas was rough, and the Playboy Mansion seemed to be the only thing that made her feel special. You could tell that she loved her time at the Mansion, despite the fact that she was constantly under watch. I felt, out of the public eye, that Trisha was scared. She wasn't necessarily happy being stuck at the Mansion every day with an extremely early curfew, but she felt as if she needed to be at the Mansion because of her past. As I mentioned, she had a very hard life in Texas, and a lot of things never seemed to work out for her. Hef was like her knight in shining armor, whisking her away from that existence. She appreciated being saved and given such a wonderful place to say. And, I'm sure, having life at the Playboy Mansion with parties and butlers was like a dream to her. Knowing Trisha, I do know how much she cared about Hef, and her intentions were always pure, but there weren't many people she could trust. Not to mention, Trisha found out that she had the breast cancer gene, so she scheduled a double mastectomy and went through months of painful surgeries to cure it during her time at the Mansion. So, she brought in a friend that she knew could be on her side.

Trisha requested from Hef that Chelsea Ryan be brought in as a girlfriend. From what I heard, Chelsea was never Hef's favorite, but he agreed to appease Trisha. Because of this, the spring and summer of 2012 was definitely a time to remember at the Playboy Mansion for me. I looked back on what it was like being in Russell's crew and was disgusted that I was ever around them at all. Now, somehow, I had magically gone from that desperate group of "wannabes" to the elite group at the Playboy Mansion.

At this point, it was the summer of 2012. Damian and I had just moved from our apartment to a nice home in the valley. He had stopped waiting tables and began working marketing on top of his Indie film endeavors. We were excited to be upgrading our lives in a cozy little house, and we were on track to be married on December 21st. Things were going very well for us. During this time, I had been blessed with a job at Bench Warmer International. With Bench Warmer, I didn't have the time to keep my brand ambassador job, so I stopped doing that, and my primary job became Bench Warmer. Bench Warmer cards are collectible trading cards with models on them rather than sports heroes. They serve as a way for fans of these models to collect memorabilia of them. It was at this time that I began modeling for Bench Warmer, as well as helping out with the production of the cards when need be. I would, occasionally, run signings where the models would come in and sign the trading cards. You see, a majority of the models for Bench Warmer were Playmates, so I would see and work with the same people that I had fun with at the mansion regularly. Aside from that, I never had a set schedule. It was completely random, and I had the freedom to set up my own hours so I could work around my endeavors at the Mansion. Because of that, I spent a lot of time at FITS this summer. In fact, it was the only summer I spent consistently at FITS

Every Sunday, Hef would come sit outside at the same table in the corner by the pool and play backgammon with Joel. The giant, cushioned pool chair next to Hef's table was, clearly, big enough for several girls, and Hef's girlfriends, Trisha and Chelsea, would sit there. (Shera didn't seem to come around a lot at this point, and Anna had Sundays with her family, so I only ever saw Chelsea and Trisha.) Then, there was another big, cushioned pool chair next to that one. That is where I found myself every Sunday. I would come down and hang out with Trisha and Chelsea. We would lay around, play in the pool or the grotto, and talk about nonsense. Generally, Jan, Alicia, and some of the new Playmates would come and hang by the pool with us, which made the day even more fun. That year, Pamela Horton (the soon-to-be Miss October 2012) had become a good friend of mine. She was living in Kansas, but she came out a few times for FITS, and it was always great to have her hang out with us. Raquel Pomplun was also a new Playmate at the time (Miss April 2012), so she would make appearances with the crew as well. We had such amazing times. We could find the humor in anything. For instance, someone had turned on the radio in the grotto when I was hanging out with Chelsea and Trisha one day, and an infomercial for a "micro-fiber mop" went on and on, and, for some reason, we got a kick out of that and joked about it for a long time. It was just the most random thing to hear repeating itself in the grotto.

I have to say, even though it seems silly, I loved it. That was my favorite time period at the Mansion. I cherish those days. All the general FITS girls who would come to visit (or who were regulars that weren't me, Jan, or Alicia) would sit and stare at us, longing to be one of us girls lucky enough to sit next to Hef and be in with the girlfriends. I never really thought of it that way, because Trisha and Chelsea were my friends. I legitimately liked them and had a good time with them, but I realized what was going on very quickly when girls we didn't know would come over and try to talk to us or just stare from afar. And I had some of the girls mention to me years later that that was how they felt. It was like we were the popular girls in school that everyone was afraid to talk to. They saw us as royalty at the Playboy Mansion. Again, it was silly, but it was also nice to be looked up to. If I could go back and tell my teenage self where I would be in a few years, I would never have believed it. I appreciated the blessing that had been bestowed on me, and I swore to never take it for granted.

One night during this summer, I tweeted Hef, "@hughhefner I can't wait until movie night tomorrow!! It's always a highlight of my week!" Suddenly, I had followers coming in from left and right. With that, I realized that Hef had retweeted me. He never did that. He only re-posted tweets from friends, Playmates, or girlfriends, and it was incredibly rare. I was excited and honored. It was most likely because the girls liked me that he did that. I gained about 200 followers within an hour because of the re-tweet. This wasn't the last time he'd do this, either. It was a silly thing to be excited over, but it was still a nice experience for me. It was right around this point in my Mansion experience where I truly had found my place.

Around this time, a girl came up to test for Playmate. I felt bad for her because she was extremely over-excited, and no one appreciated that. She took photos of everyone while they were eating, video-taped everything, and tried to talk Hef's ear off while he was playing backgammon (which is a big no-no). She was a beautiful girl, but of course, she didn't make Playmate. She was too clingy and obnoxious for Hef, and the odds were that he remembered her personality upon reviewing her centerfold test. I felt bad for her because I understood why she was excited, but being that desperate is never good. I always remember that moment and how bad I felt for that poor girl.

There was another girl, around this time, that got picked to be a Playmate. She came in town to shoot her centerfold and spent days shooting to get it right. She was never able to create that perfect image that Hef wanted, and the title of Playmate was, more or less, taken back. They rejected her centerfold and sent her back home. That was the first time I saw that happen, but from what I heard, it became more common later.

It was sad hearing about all the distressing news of girls not making Playmate, but one definite perk of being in the "in crowd" at the Mansion was all the little secrets that you found out. For instance, I knew who the Playmate of the Year was months before it was announced. I found out that Brittany Nola, Miss November 2012, did not actually make Playmate. She tested and was turned down by Hef. When a girl whose issue was about to hit the stands dropped her title because her boyfriend made her, Nola became a Playmate. (I can say that she has Joel and Alison to thank for influencing Hef's decision to make her a Playmate when the almost-Playmate fell through.) I saw girls screw themselves out of Playmate of the Year by badmouthing Hef. (They'll probably never know that they were up for the running, either.) One day, I heard Ray Anthony say that he was upset that Hef hadn't truly smiled for years. Those things were interesting to hear, but to no real extent did they hurt anyone.

Plus, I loved being able to hear from and pick the brains of those so deeply invested in the history of the brand. Alison had so many stories from her history with the company, and they were always interesting to me. Richard would get into debates with people on ideas and theories, and I found it fascinating to just observe. The roots of Playboy were at the dinner table with me each night, and I couldn't help but feel blessed to listen to their ideas and appreciate the company that I had been so graciously invited into. I was becoming very educated on Playboy and its working and ideologies.

On top of that, I loved getting to watch and meet celebrities. Jon Lovitz was a frequent Mansion regular, as was Corey Feldman and even Michelle Trachtenberg, Bella Lugosi Jr, and Chris Evans stopped by while I was around. I had a growing collection of celebrity photos featuring me with Gene Simmons, Kendra, Lakers players, and many more. That mixed in with the fun I was having with Trisha and all my friends, life at the Mansion was looking up. Then, the inevitable happened.

# The Return of the Future Mrs. Hefner

Suddenly, Shera stopped showing her face. There was a week or so where we didn't see her. Hef said that she was on a vacation and we all, more or less, forgot about it. Then, it happened. After a year of being away, Crystal Harris was back. Out of nowhere, I went to a Friday movie night, and Alicia turned to me and said, "Did you hear that Crystal's back?"

I froze, "No way."

Alicia said, "It's true. Check your twitter."

It was true. Crystal had tweeted, "Yes @hughhefner and I are back together. Yes I am his #1 girl again. Yes we are happy. Hope that clears up any confusion! Xo"

Hef followed this up with, "Getting back together with Crystal Harris shouldn't be a big surprise, since I have a history of remaining close to former girlfriends. Shera is in Canada visiting her family, which is unrelated to Crystal being here. Shera & my other Mansion girlfriends welcomed Crystal here at dinner on Tuesday night, before playing games together. It's Mary O'Connor that brought Crystal Harris back. Crystal was miserable & said so Mary told Crystal to write & tell me, which she did."

So, that was it. Crystal came crawling back to Hef. It didn't affect my life too much at first, seeing as how she never came down for FITS, and she only came down right before movies at movie night. However, it did deeply affect the lives of the girlfriends. Unlike what Hef tweeted, Shera did not come back. She was promptly moved into the Bunny House with Crystal's return. We saw very little of her around after that. For all I knew, though, she was moved into the bunny house before Crystal even returned, as we hadn't seen her for about a week prior.

Anna was Crystal's best friend for a long time. They even remained friends after Crystal had left Hef before the wedding. I was told that Crystal, when she realized how bad off she was away from the Mansion, went to Anna and asked her to see if Hef would take her back. Hef, of course, was disgusted by the idea. Anna, then, told him how much happier she would be if Crystal was at the Mansion with her again, since they were such good friends. Crystal wrote Hef a letter, and, with help from Anna's persuasion, he allowed Crystal to come back. According to Anna, upon arriving back, Crystal immediately turned on Anna and pointed out to Hef that she had a boyfriend, providing enough proof that Hef couldn't doubt the situation. Crystal told Hef that she wanted Anna gone because she was a "liar." When he confronted Anna about it, she was over the situation. She gladly moved out, knowing that it was better not to live with someone who could stab their best friend in the back. According to Crystal, the office found out that Anna was cheating on Hef and made her leave while Crystal was on a trip in Australia, and she knew nothing of it. Knowing Crystal, however, "the office" was always a front to hide her wrong-doings. Regardless, Anna was gone for good.

At first, with Trisha, Crystal seemed to be playing nice. Like always, I watched from a distance, as I was weary from what I was told about her before she left. I was told to be scared of Crystal, and I was sure it was for a good reason. Crystal played nice and took Trisha to Disney; they hung out a bit, and life seemed fine. I would hang out with Trisha whenever Crystal was not around.

For instance, one of the few times Crystal was at FITS, she was talking politely with Trisha on their lawn chairs. She came over and offered me a frozen grape, and I took one and thanked her. Aside from that, she wanted nothing to do with me, so I just laid out on my own. Once Crystal went upstairs, Trisha called me over and we hung out for the rest of the day. She knew that I was smart to stay distanced from Crystal.

It didn't take more than a month for Crystal to stop playing it safe, and she took the Mansion back over. Trisha and Chelsea were too meek for her, and Anna and Shera were gone. From what it seemed, girls that she didn't like were thrown out left and right. She was surrounding herself with a group of girls that she was comfortable with, and I could tell. Trisha actually approached me one day to tell me that girls were getting cut, frequently. She told me that she would not let this happen to me. She told me to tell her if I ever got cut, and she would take care of it. She was so sweet. That being said, I knew it was only a matter of time before Crystal got rid of the last two girlfriends. Chelsea only lasted until the end of the summer. Chelsea had her eyes set on Playmate, and that was the only reason she was around. Crystal saw that and helped her get a Playmate test to expedite the process. Chelsea tested for Playmate, without Hef knowing, and he found out and told her that she probably wouldn't get it. He did, however, get her a new car. The next day, Chelsea told Hef that it wasn't working out. She was gone, and you could see Crystal's hold on Hef getting stronger.

Trisha held out for a long time. She didn't want to go back to her life in Texas, and I did not blame her. She felt even more, however, like she was always being watched. She was wise to think that, as I'm sure Crystal was always watching her. She had to leave the Mansion to walk her dog to talk on the phone. She had to watch everything she said. She was not only dealing with the idea that anyone and everyone could be against her, but she was also going through her double mastectomy at this time. And, slowly but surely, Crystal began to be colder and colder to her.

The next thing I knew, it was October. I was sitting at the dinner table on a Friday night talking to Caya. Caya began bashing Trisha to me, saying that she was awkward and that she and Crystal didn't like her. It became worse and worse. Just recently, Caya had been Trisha's friend. Not anymore. From that point on, I heard, daily, how awkward and horrible Trisha was from Caya, Crystal, and a lot of the Mansion girls. It broke my heart. This sweet girl underwent serious surgery, and Crystal and Caya were making her life a living hell during the process. I did nothing but keep my mouth shut and ignore the nonsense. I refused to say anything negative about Trisha. I just tuned out what I was hearing, as speaking out would have only made things harder for Trisha.

At this same time, Alicia and Caya were becoming better friends. Alicia was consistently trying to get me to go out with her, but everything that she wanted to do I wasn't fond of. She was single, so she wanted to be out where the party was. I was engaged, and I wanted to stay at home and hang out. Because of this, we really only had our Mansion attendance as a common bond. We were not the same type of person, otherwise. I loved seeing her and talking to her at the Mansion, but I wasn't about to go out into the clubbing scene again. She began to get a little disgruntled that I wouldn't go out with her. I didn't think it was a big deal, but it was something that came up later.

I began to fear not just for Trisha, but for the lifestyle that I had been used to as well. I always appreciated the time that I had at the Mansion and knew that it would not last. However, I was not ready to drop all of this and stop attending yet. I loved my life at home with my husband and our cat, but the Mansion became something that was mine. I didn't really have any true girlfriends in LA outside of Playboy. This became the only social life that I had, and it brought me joy to be around all of these people. What would happen to me if I lost all of that? My husband has always been my best friend, but having girlfriends was something that I loved. It wasn't easy for me to make friends, and the friends I found at the Mansion made me comfortable. I just hoped that things wouldn't change too much for me yet.

# Hef's Third Marriage

Finally, in December of 2012, it was announced that Hef and Crystal were to be married (for real this time) on New Year's Eve. The New Year's party would serve as their reception. My heart sank. I feared not just for my future at the Mansion, but for Trisha's as well, and for how things would change. I knew that some of the horrible rumors I heard about Crystal weren't true, but some were. If she was to take over as Hef's wife, how much would things actually change? I hoped they wouldn't. Trisha told me that Hef and Crystal said she was welcomed to stay after they got married, and she was very grateful for that.

During that month, I went home for Christmas and for my own wedding. Damian and I were married on December 21, 2012 in a manor house in Williamsburg, Virginia. It was a small winter ceremony, but I was so happy with it. The night before the wedding, we actually stayed at a plantation that was featured on the show *Ghost Hunters*, and that was a highlight of the vacation. The commotion of my wedding and Christmas distracted me from the drama that was going down at the Mansion, but, it couldn't delete what was about to happen.

The Hefner wedding went on as planned. Hef and Crystal were married in the daytime on December 31, 2012, and that night we all celebrated the event at the New Year's party. As I attended the reception, I searched the crowds for Trisha. She wasn't there. Trisha was nowhere to be found, and that worried me. I truly thought of her as a friend, and I was pained by all she was going through. She did not need the drama that was thrown at her.

Over the next few weeks, I saw Caya post on Facebook, "A Marriage is between TWO PEOPLE living in one house together...with no one else." I knew what that was about. It was awful, but it spurred memories in my head from Russell and Vanessa. That night when Kristina was yelling at them, "a relationship is between TWO PEOPLE," played over and over in my mind. Talk about irony. Caya continued to tell me the same thing during movie nights. She didn't care that Trisha might be able to hear her, as she was only a few spots away. It was sad because Caya had paraded herself around as Trisha's friend for the longest time. Now, the tides had turned.

Of course, within a month, Trisha had to pack up her bags and leave. I had heard that Crystal told Hef that they were married, and that meant two people in a house. He gave in, and Trisha was sent back home to Texas, immediately after recovering from her final surgery. The day before she left, Trisha said to me, "I'm really going to miss you, Malorie. You're one of the only true people here." And I missed her, too. Things at the Mansion weren't as fun without her there... at least not for a long time. Having Trisha at the Mansion was a guarantee that I would always have a friend present for movie nights. I no longer had that guarantee.

In fact, once Crystal took over as Mrs. Hefner, the lady of the Manor, things took a scary turn. Mary O'Connor passed away. Mary had been Hef's secretary for many, many years. Playboy wouldn't have been what it was without Mary. Hef's health, at this time, took a turn for the worst. Something got infected in his mouth, and he was bedridden for almost a month. He canceled a few movie nights and stopped reading movie notes before the Friday movies that he did attend. Things were not looking good.

With Hef's illness came a scary, inevitable fear that Playboy would never be the same. Girls were no longer welcomed to stay at the Bunny House (the property next door that housed the Playmates who moved out to LA), and it seemed as if this was a bad omen. It created a fear in everyone that Hef would not make it and that life as they knew it would change. Everyone was worried, but no one would say anything. Fortunately, Hef recovered from the illness after a long mourning period over Mary. His spirits seemed to be slightly up, and he was in better health again. Aside from being naturally frail and old, he seemed fine. And, despite all the negative, horrible things people said about Crystal Hefner, I have to say that she made that man very happy. And that's all that matters, right? She made him the happiest I'd ever seen him, and she made herself comfortable as Mrs. Hefner. She weeded out all the girls she didn't like, and life seemed to be, yet again, stagnant at the Mansion. Crystal had found her place, and things settled down. The concern about the Bunny House being closed because of Hef's illness seemed to be just a worry. It turned out that all the girls were asked to move out, not because of Hef's health, but because he was selling it. In its place, he bought Crystal a five-million-dollar house to live in in Malibu after he passed away. At this time, I knew that Hef was doing better, and Crystal had fully settled in. Who knew what my journey at the Mansion would lead to next?

MALORIE MACKEY

# Part 3:
# The Chaos of the Playboy Mansion

MALORIE MACKEY

# Crystal & Club 33

As I mentioned before, on December 31, 2012, Crystal Harris and Hugh Hefner were united in Holy Matrimony. I won't say that many people were happy about it, but Crystal made Hef happy in a way that I had never seen before, and that's all that matters, right?

For me, married life seemed to be the same old thing that I was comfortable with. Damian and I came back from Virginia after our wedding, and our house and work were in the same state that we had left them in. Plus, Damian and I had lived together for years before the marriage and we already knew everything about each other, so of course we were happy with the way things were. Nothing changed at my home, but that wasn't the case at the Mansion.

Shortly after Hef and Crystal were married, things at the Mansion drastically quieted down. Girls who would normally come to try and hook up with Hef or who came with the dream that they could be a "Girl Next Door" stopped coming. Others who used to come up for fun were scared away because of the fear they had for Crystal. It was known that Crystal banned many girls from the Mansion. A lot of girls thought it was better to remove themselves from the list by not showing up rather than to be blacklisted.

The Mansion was becoming more and more of a ghost town. Girls thought that they were being smart by avoiding Crystal, but I realized something about her. It seemed that she surrounded herself with people she liked and was comfortable with. People she didn't want to see were kicked out. By the time Crystal and Hef had their six-month anniversary, if you were still at the house, you were safe (unless Crystal wanted to become better friends with you-which almost never happened).

For those of us who were just in it for the relaxing times that we could have at the Mansion with friends, things still changed. The few friends we had were either gone completely or rarely came. Trisha had been sent home, at Crystal's request, as soon as Hef and Crystal were married. I would come up on FITS Sundays to find that it was only me, Joel, Alison, Hef, and Marston. The men would play backgammon while Alison and I chatted. But that was starting to get boring. I would come up Friday nights because I loved the relaxing atmosphere of the twenty or so people having dinner and watching classic movies, plus I got to see Alicia, who I enjoyed hanging out with at the Mansion. There was a long period of time when even she had left, so I felt very alone. Don't get me wrong, I loved Joel and Alison. I loved talking to Richard and Ray Anthony, but it was not quite the same without a friend my own age to spend time with.

During May of 2013, Damian and I booked an Indie film that was shooting in Prague, Oklahoma. For a month, we were staying at a farm house in the middle of nowhere. Prague had one traffic light in the entire town, and you could almost count the number of establishments in the area on one hand. (I would drive 45 minutes to get to Starbucks when I wanted coffee.) It was a great experience, though, as we got to work with John Schneider from *The Dukes of Hazzard*, and I was able to herd cattle during this adventure. Plus, I was acting in the film, so it was great to add this to my resume. And, of course, being away from Los Angeles for a month meant being away from the Mansion for a month.

When I came back, I felt obligated (and also excited) to walk back into the Playboy Mansion. I texted Alicia the morning of Friday, May 31st and asked, "Are you going up to the Mansion tonight? I'm finally back! I can't wait to see you!"

Alicia replied, "No, I'm busy moving into my new place today."

At the time, I was upset by this statement. I knew that I had to go to the Mansion because I hadn't been in a long time. They noticed in the office when we stopped showing up a lot, and I always heard that you would face the possibility of getting removed from the list upon not coming up as frequently as they would like. I needed to show my face, but I was a little disheartened without having another girl there. Little did I know, that was the best thing that could have happened to me on that particular day. (And possibly the worst for what it eventually led to.)

As I pulled up the long driveway, I was relieved to see that security still recognized my face. I saw the side of the Mansion and pulled around and forward up to the familiar manor. When I stepped inside, I laid my bag down on the cushion to the far right of the movie screen, as I always did. I traced my steps back out of the movie room, across the great hall, and into the dining room. In the dining room, I found Crystal and Richard sitting alone together, each in their regular seats at the large main table, talking. I came in, and Richard greeted me, "Malorie! Long time no see."

I replied back and also said "Hi" to Crystal. They both began asking me about where I had been and what I had been through. I told them the story of the wild tornado on the last day of our filming and how we blew up a house one day on set. This was the longest conversation I had had with Crystal to date. (I should have been scared, because I knew it was never good for her to notice you.) Then, somehow, the topic of my birthday came up. Crystal was being incredibly nice to me and seemed genuinely interested in what I had to say. This was surprising to me because, from what I knew about her, she never really got to know people and was very stand-offish. She seemed to get easily annoyed with girls trying to be her friend, and she wanted nothing to do with most of the girls that come around. Luckily, she knew I was married, and I think that helped her feel more comfortable around me. My guess was that she also liked me because she knew I worked with Bench Warmer, which was something she modeled for at the time, and I was always quiet and stand-offish from her, which I'm sure she appreciated. As we began bringing up my birthday (which was the following week), Charlie, her King Charles Cavalier, jumped up and put his front paws on the dinner buffet and began licking a stick of butter. We all enjoyed a good laugh from that as Crystal pulled him off the table and threw away the licked butter. I told her that I would be going to Disneyland for my birthday and asked her if there was anything I should do in particular while I was there, knowing that she was a Disney fanatic.

"I could make you a reservation at Club 33. Would you want me to do that for you?" She smiled at me.

I couldn't believe what I heard. With that, we exchanged numbers. I told her that I would love that, and I'd text her the following day with the information.

I'm assuming that not everyone knows about Club 33. Almost everyone I know is either a fanatic about Club 33 or has never heard of it. Club 33 is a secret club in Disneyland. It was created by Walt Disney as a place where he could treat corporate investors. It was named Club 33 because its address is 33 Royal Street in Disneyland, and because Disney originally had 33 corporate investors who were invited to join the club. It opened just five weeks after Walt Disney passed away. Even though he never saw it, he had much to do with the club's design. Later, membership was opened to the public.

In order to join Club 33, one must be put on a waiting list that is rumored to be between 2 to 14 years long, and it closes very frequently. Most recently, a cast member told me that the waiting list had grown to 30 years long. There are a couple of different membership levels, but, for the largest level at the time when Crystal joined, one had to pay over $25,000 to be a part of the club, and they had to pay annual dues rumored to be $11,000 a year. Crystal had to get the most expensive level (the platinum level) to join when she did. Needless to say, this secret place is only for the rich or famous, and the fact that Crystal offered to get me a reservation was such a wonderful thing. I had always wanted to go to Club 33. It is a once-in-a-lifetime opportunity for most people, and I was happy to take her up on it.

Before this, I wasn't very fond of Crystal. She had never done anything mean to me, but I had seen her be vicious towards other girls, so I was definitely worried about getting too close to her. Her reputation among the FITS girls wasn't a very good one. After this, my opinion of her changed. I had nothing bad to say anymore. She went out of her way to do something nice for me, and I was grateful for it. However, I should have thought about everything that I knew about her. She had noticed me, and that could never end well. Regardless, I was going to enjoy the kindness that she offered me.

On June 8, 2013, Damian and I went to Disneyland. For my birthday, he had commissioned a custom-made replica of one of Evita Peron's dresses for me. I wore it to the park, excited about going to Club 33. We arrived at the Club just in time for lunch. At the time, the Club 33 door was discretely placed in between a shop entrance and the Blue Bayou entrance. There was nothing on the door but a sign that said, "33." We lifted the knob on the speaker and rang the doorbell. A hostess came from the inside with her book and said, "Reservation? Can I have your last name?" Once we gave her our last name, she opened the door, and we walked inside this wonderful, magical place.

The carpets in the entrance foyer were red, as were the walls. It looked like a beautiful, French-style Victorian home. In the middle of the room sat a vintage French lift. The lady asked us if we would like to take the lift upstairs, and, of course, we said yes! We got in the French lift, she took our photo, and we rode the lift up to the second floor. The lift was gorgeous; it was made out of dark brown wood, and you could see through the design as we rode up to the second floor. Upon the lift stopping, another hostess opened the door for us and let us out into the hallway of the upstairs. Straight ahead of us, I could see the Trophy room. This was a small room made to be a banquet area for parties. You could see fake animals decorated around the room and a notorious vulture in the corner of it. This vulture was part of an old system Disney had set up. The plan was that while investors ate in there, microphones would be placed around so an employee hiding in a microphone room could listen in on conversations and then reply and interrupt as the voice of a mechanical animal in the room. This was never completed (I'm sure for the sake of everyone's privacy), but we could still see the microphones and the vulture in the corner. From there, we were led down the lounge hallway passed the bar, then further down passed the buffets to our seats.

The main dining hall was decorated to look like an elegant plantation home, perfectly fitting the New Orleans section of Disneyland that it was found in. The club actually stretched around most of the second story of the New Orleans' streets. Dark blue and ivory curtains draped to the floor off of all of the full-size window/doors that led you out onto the balcony. Damian and I sat at a two-person table by one of the windows, and it was beautiful. We both ordered the salmon, and we were able to go to the appetizer buffet, which was decorated with shrimp, crab, fruits, and salads. Across from the appetizer buffet was the dessert buffet, which we visited later. After our salmon arrived, we took a break before dessert and went out onto the balconies. There were two different balconies on opposite sides of the main room. I went to the first and looked out and down on all the people walking through Disneyland. It was crazy that of the thousands at the park, we were one of six tables in the club. We then looked at all the staged balconies across from us, which were dressed beautifully. I went back inside and exited to the second balcony. From that balcony, you could see the big lake and, around the side, you could see the Club 33 entrance. Somehow, we wound up on the other side of the street from it. It made me realize how long the club was, as I hadn't noticed walking around on the inside.

When we went back in for dessert, the waitress brought me a special Mickey Mouse cake for my birthday. It was so nice! On the plate, the chef wrote, "Happy Birthday" in chocolate. I ordered a Sangria with it (because this is the only place in Disneyland Park where you can drink alcohol, and Sangria is one of the only things I will drink), and we enjoyed our dessert. After dinner, we went back down the long buffet and lounge hall, passing pencil sketches of the Disneyland castle and other classic photos. At the end of the hall, there hung the costume design sketches for Mary Poppins. I had to get my picture with those! They were lightly-sketched images of Bert and Mary's outfits from within the paintings of the movie, and the children's sketches were down below them. Next to the paintings were the restrooms, which had wicker toilets in them.

Once we were ready to leave, we had to order merchandise to show that we had been there in this once-in-a-lifetime experience. I got Club 33 Mickey Ears, a wine glass, and a polo. Damian got two Club 33 lapel pins.

It was a magical experience, and I had Crystal Hefner to thank for that—a woman I had feared for so long; a woman who had falling outs with almost every one of her friends; a woman who was feared by many. Perhaps she wasn't so bad after all? I could do nothing but like her after she had done this for me for nothing in return. After this, Crystal Hefner began to surprise me in many ways.

Believe it or not, the next time I saw Crystal, she ignored me entirely. I was talking to her mother, and she pulled her mother away to talk to her about something. I was worried because she never gave me a chance to thank her in person. However, shortly after that, I was able to officially thank her at the July 4th party. It was definitely not how I envisioned it would go. She told me she was so glad that I had a good time and pulled Cooper over to tell him that I went there. With that, she trailed off so I would go away. It was almost like she threw me off on Cooper. It was clear that she didn't want to be friends. She just wanted to be nice and civil from time to time. I was absolutely okay with this.

# Pam and Raquel

As my life dove deeper into Playboy, I developed my own best friends. Pamela Horton was Miss October 2012; however, I met her the day that she tested for Playmate, a year before she got her Playmate title. She came up for a movie night on a night where I got lost and broke my GPS. Lucky for me, she was at the round table that night, and I joined her there because my seat at the main table was gone due to my tardiness. We hit it off so well that we exchanged numbers. I sent her photos from the scrapbooking basket when they came out, just in case she didn't make Playmate, and she called me the day that she found out that she did.

We talked through the process of her coming out to California from Kansas, and I was there when she started dating her first boyfriend in California. A year after we met, we began to hang out and have "fort nights." We would build a fort in the living room out of the couch, chairs, and blankets and have sleepovers in it while watching movies. Pam was refreshing because she acted like a child in the way that I did, so we had a lot of fun being silly together. For a while, it was just the two of us. That was until Raquel Pomplun decided to force her way in.

I knew Raquel from the Mansion, but I did not know her well. We had spent some time together on Sundays and talked a bit, but we didn't really get to know each other well until she shot for Bench Warmer. At the same time, she agreed to do our upcoming *League of Legends* parody music video that my husband was shooting. From the music video onward, we were friends. She was such an amazing person with a good heart. She always looked out for me. She joined our fort nights and fit in perfectly. That year, the three of us went to Halloween Horror Nights together and then did a fort night after. The three of us made nasty home-made face masks and laughed about it for hours. The three of us even did photo shoots together from time to time. Like every circle of friends, we had our ups and downs, but I loved hanging out with Pam and Raquel.

There was a period of time at the end of 2013 where Pam went back to Kansas for Thanksgiving. Raquel and I had a few one-on-one days that we really needed, and one of them was at Disneyland! I can't even describe how much fun Raquel and I had at Disneyland that day. Since she was PMOY, Playboy had leased her a jag, and the man at the gate for Disneyland liked her jag so much that he gave us handicapped parking, so we were right up close. I appreciated Raquel's willingness to follow me everywhere and her acceptance of the fact that I turned into a child the second we were at Disneyland. She followed me all day long, and we had a blast. At lunchtime, she took a photo by Club 33 with me. I had been, but she never had, so she made a sad face with me next to it saying, "Bucketlist. Wish I could go." Within five minutes, Crystal texted us and said, "I can get you guys in. Do you want to go for dinner?"

We spent the entire Splash Mountain ride giggling about Club 33. It was amazing. Of course, we had an issue getting in because someone messed up our reservation. When we texted Crystal, she replied back "I'm so angry right now. I can't believe they messed that up. Hef's pissed for you guys, too! I'm calling right now." The club was so apologetic and so eager to fix the situation that we got free pins, which was nice. They sat us at a small table in the Trophy Room, which I loved since I hadn't gotten to sit in that dining room before.

We felt awful for having to bother Crystal about the mix-up (and both of us were still, partly, scared of her), but she was so nice to me in the car ride home when I texted her that I knew everything was okay. I had been to Club 33 once at lunch and once at dinner. I had been to Club 33 and dined in both dining rooms. And, now, every time I wore my Club 33 ears to Disney, all the employees wanted to ask me about it. It was pretty amazing. Not to mention, I was on good terms with Crystal, my best friends were awesome, and I really did feel on top of the world.

Over time, Raquel and I grew to be the best of friends. We were still friends with Pamela, but the two of us grew closer and closer together. We became almost inseparable, and she, truly, transformed into one of the few people that I felt completely comfortable around in LA. I could be myself, and she loved me for who I was.

As our friendship developed, we realized that we weren't working together as much as we liked. Raquel called me one morning to say, "I have an idea! Let's be the next Tina Fey and Amy Poehler!" And, with that, our comedy duo was formed. We decided to create a comedy web series, forging ourselves into *Chocolate Milk*. With our show, we saw each other more and more. Whenever we weren't hanging out, we would be developing content with Damian (who became the director) for our sketches.

Throughout all of my endeavors through the end of my time at the Mansion, she was there for me. And she has continued to be there for me to this day. If I could say I got one amazing thing out of my time at the Mansion, it was definitely my friendship with Raquel.

# Marston

During one movie night, I got an invitation from Joel and Alison to do a pub crawl directly after the movie. Damian was, of course, invited, as they had been trying to get him to come out for months. They had invited us out several times before, but I had always been too busy to attend, so I felt obligated to go this time. I left movie night early to pick up Damian and went back over the hill to meet Joel and Alison. I knew that Morgan Farrington (Hef's nephew) and Alicia were both going to be there, but they were the only people I knew who would be attending aside from Joel and Alison. As Damian and I approached the Rainbow Bar and Grill where the crawl began, I saw Joel and Alison sitting outside at a patio table. They were sitting with Marston, Hef's second-youngest son, and his new girlfriend.

We pulled up, said our hellos, and Joel and Alison began telling Marston about the big movie that we had just been on as Damian showed them the videos we had of us blowing up a house. Slowly but surely, Alicia and Morgan came to join us at the table. As we ate, Damian connected with Morgan and Marston about how much they loved video games. He seemed to fit in with them. That night, we hopped from the Rainbow, to the Roxy, to Rock and Reilly's, to a private booth at The

Viper Room. Joel and Alison seemed to know everyone everywhere and were easily able to get us from place to place.

Now, upon first impression, Marston Hefner comes off very shy. He doesn't talk much, and he seems slightly stand-offish. Because of that, Damian didn't think he made any impression on him that night.

To Damian's surprise, the morning after the pub crawl, he received an invitation to Marston's own movie night. Marston had friended him on Facebook and invited him to the event. When I checked my Facebook, I was surprised to see that he had invited me as well. I was even more surprised to see that we would be attending the event at the Playboy Mansion.

Truth be told, I was really excited. My husband finally got to come to the Playboy Mansion, which was a big part of my life. He could finally see everything for himself, and he was invited in the most random way. Minus a few exceptions, none of the other girls could ever bring their men except, maybe, to a large party. It was pretty insane. I was very excited for him, even though he didn't seem to think one way or another about getting to go.

So, the more and more I developed relationships in LA, the more my entire life wound up revolving around Playboy. My weekend fun was at the Mansion. In my line of work with Bench Warmer, I modeled and worked with tons of Playmates on a daily basis; my best friend was PMOY, and now my husband was satellite to that world, as he was becoming friends with Marston.

We went up to Marston's movie night on July 27, 2013. I pulled up to the intercom with Damian and was greeted by one of my security buds. We drove up the long driveway, and Damian got his first glance at the Playboy Mansion. As we pulled up, Marston greeted us at the door and gave us both hugs. We went in the dining room and sat around the table, meeting Marston's other friends who came out to enjoy *Dead Snow* with us.

We talked, caught up, and ordered tea and drinks for the movie. From the moment that Marston and Damian began chatting, you could tell that they were going to be friends. Marston brought up the video game *Super Smash Brothers*, and Damian responded with excitement, thus sealing their friendship.

As we all gathered around the movie room to watch *Dead Snow* on the big screen, Damian and I looked for the best seat. We began to head towards a couch up to the side of the wall when Marston said, "No, it's much better here. Sit here," as he patted the empty seat next to him on his couch. Now, this spot is normally Hef's movie seat, but, seeing as it was Marston's movie, this was his seat tonight, and he had just invited Damian and me to sit on the couch with him. This was a big deal. Most people would think that I'm crazy talking about a couch like this, but Hugh Hefner is a man of habit. His chair is sacred to him, and it's generally just him and his girlfriends who sit there. The fact that Marston pulled us up on the couch for his movie was an extremely kind gesture.

I continued to see Marston on Sundays at the Mansion after that night. Sometimes Marston seemed to be strangely intimidating to girls at the Mansion. Most people were put off by his what-seemed-to-be "cold" attitude. I believed that Marston was a good person with good intentions. I believed that he could be stand-offish, and that was why some people were put off by him. His viewpoints could sometimes be that of someone brought up in a high-society atmosphere, but that's why, I think, we were able to be such good friends. Damian and I came from a liberal group, all living together, roughing it out in LA to follow our art and our dreams. When Marston called out certain points, we were quick to debate him on them. Being a philosophy major, he liked to debate, and I think we opened up his mind on a few subjects, or at least got him to hear arguments from another side. And he did the same for us. But, on other topics, Marston could be very open-minded. In fact, he and Damian were very similar in that regard.

Marston was also a very passionate and intelligent man. He was an amazing writer, and he strove to always be the best he could be in anything he did—like no one I've seen before. Damian and I are blessed to call him a friend. As a friend, he has supported all of Damian's and my endeavors.

Within a month, Marston began frequenting our home. At least once a week I would come home to him, Damian, and two of our roommates playing *Super Smash Brothers* on the couch. They'd be screaming, cursing, and laughing with each other. This became a pretty common thing, and Marston would bring Damian to Smash tournaments a lot. (Damian has always been really good at *Super Smash Brothers,* but when he would hang out with Marston, he would come home grumbling about how Marston could kick his butt because he was that much better at the game than Damian was.) I also really enjoyed the time Damian and I spent out double dating with Marston. We never did anything too crazy, but going to dinner and a movie was something that was fun for me.

A few months into our friendship, Marston did the one thing that I thought wasn't possible: he convinced Damian to go out to the Playboy Mansion parties with us. I tried a few times to get Damian to want to go to the big events in the past, but it wasn't really his thing. However, when he felt Marston really wanted him to do it, he roughed it up and did it. (I say "roughed it up," but you know it's never that hard to convince a guy to make it out to the Playboy parties.)

Damian was living a dream, and he didn't even realize it. I had been going to the Playboy Mansion for three plus years at this point. His first event was my third Halloween Party, and, sure, I always got to park at the Mansion and go early for the movie, but he had it even better. We met Marston and his girlfriend at Marston's mother's house around 4pm. Marston said, "So, we did not get up today. Do you guys want to come with us to get our costumes or go watch the movie at the Mansion before the party?"

I replied with, "It's up to you."

"Okay. Let's see if I can drop you off, and I will go out. That way you guys don't have to miss the movie." I thought it was slightly bizarre that he wanted to drop us off at 4:20pm, seeing how dinner didn't even start or open up until 5pm, but I didn't say anything. Maybe he knew something I didn't? We arrived at the gate where security let us all up. Marston was surprised not to see anyone, so he asked for the movie time. Once he was told 6:30pm, he announced that he thought it was 4:30pm, so he made the decision to have us go shopping with them. With that decision, I needed to change out of my home-made Frankenweenie outfit, seeing as it was a little too scandalous for the public. (The top was a sweatshirt, but the bottoms were boyshorts, and I was not about to go out in public in underwear.) So, his girlfriend took me by the hand and brought me upstairs to their room. The boys followed. This was surreal for me. For three years I'd been at the Mansion, and I had never gone upstairs. No one goes upstairs in this day and age unless they live there or work there... and Damian got to go upstairs on his second visit, clueless to how crazy this actually was. Not that it was unheard of, but there had barely been any girls living there in the past three years, and Hef was getting old, so the upstairs was, more or less, shut down to the majority of people.

We rounded up the curved staircase and turned left at the top to head down the hall. We passed Hef's room and rounded left again, heading down the small hallway. We passed cabinets with statues and artwork, inevitably arriving at the room at the very end of the hall—Marston's room whenever he wanted to stay.

The room had white walls, a nice love seat by the window with salmon colored curtains, a very beautiful, old-style bed with dark wood, and a very spacious bathroom of its own. And, in the corner, was a cute little wooden desk with a bunny-shaped seat. The floor was wooden, and I really liked the style. I had heard girls complain about the age of the rooms, but I really liked the old-style look. It was classy in my opinion.

Once in the room, I changed into a dress that his girlfriend had and, for the first time in my life, I went out in a dress without underwear on (the underwear I was wearing for my costume had a tail sewn on it because I was Frankenweenie). I was so uncomfortable. We went to Target to get saran wrap to cover his girlfriend with (as she was a Dexter victim for her costume), then we went to another costume store and to a hookah bar for Marston. I held the skirt of the dress the whole time that we were out because it bothered me so much. I felt so exposed, even though I wasn't, and I felt like I was going to get sick because of the draft. I learned that day that that style is not for me.

We made it back to the Mansion just in time for the movie. We watched "Young Frankenstein" and, following the movie, we went upstairs to help saran wrap Marston's girlfriend for her costume. Once we were all ready, we went downstairs where Hef and Crystal were taking their pictures.

Now, at that time, despite the fact that Crystal was becoming more and more friendly with me, I knew that she could be temperamental. She was sweet to me, but I was still cautious. I was definitely still intimidated by her. I was afraid that my presence upstairs and later in Hef's cabana would be off-putting to her, but she actually didn't seem to mind it. Before we went outside for the party, she took a photo of herself and Hef in their costumes and was asking me my opinion for the Instagram filter. Once we went out for the party, Marston brought us into Hef's cabana briefly, and she waved very kindly at us and told Damian how great it was to finally meet him. She was extremely nice to him.

Damian did not realize it, but he was one of the few men to ever be in Hef's cabana with him. In my time, the only men in his cabana were family. His friends did not even come in except to say "Hi." And here was my husband and myself with Hef in his cabana. And, just like that, Damian got to meet him. Of course at this point, Hef was 87 years old, so he went up after about thirty minutes of the party, so Cooper and Marston took over the cabana with all the Playmates right after he went up. Damian and I spent the party hanging out with Marston, my best friends (Pam and Raquel), and all the other girls that I worked with and saw regularly. It was a great night, and I know, even though he doesn't like parties, that Damian did have a good time. I couldn't wait for him to experience the July 4th event the following year.

On July 4th, 2014, Hef's mind was still well, but his body was not. He had to get back surgery, and it kept him from walking. Because of this, all of the FITS Sundays took place inside the library. Hef had long since been able to walk to the game house, so he stayed in the main house. Now, it was too much for him to go to the back yard, so he played in the library. We would come in and get photos with him, say our hellos, and then go out and lay by the pool without Hef's presence. The Mansion became less and less. It was becoming a shadow of what it once was. All that we would once look forward to was slowly going away. It was around this time that Hef stopped reading the movie notes on Friday nights, as well. We hoped that Hef would make it outside for July 4th, but no one was sure this would be a reality. He did wind up making it out; however, it was too far for him to walk to the pool with his back the way it was, so he sat at the table closest to the Mansion's entrance to play backgammon outside.

Damian and I went to meet Marston at his mom's house before heading over to the party. Once everyone was ready, we pulled up to the gate and went up that long driveway once more. On the steep hill coming down the side of the house, we could see that giant, patriotic slip and slide that I was looking forward to, as I did every year. We parked, got our wrist bands, and headed into the party. For the first couple of hours, Marston had to play backgammon with Hef, so Damian and I were left to hang out. I showed him the zoo, the pool, the grotto, and everything he hadn't seen before. Once Marston had gotten done with backgammon, Raquel and her husband arrived, as did Pamela and her boyfriend. I was worried that it would be hard for me to balance my husband with my Playmate friends, as my husband was hanging out with Marston the whole time since he was Marston's guest. Luckily, it worked out better than I could have imagined. Not only was Damian having such a good time with Marston, but there were four guys to play beer pong, so the girls could spend time together. It was an amazing day swimming, slip and sliding, and running all over the backyard. By the end of the day, Raquel had way too much to drink. She lost it, and I took care of her until she crawled down into the gym and hid so she could pass out. Once the spectacular fireworks display finished, I had to round up Pamela, Raquel, their significant others, and my husband (as I was the only one who didn't drink). We wound up going back on the shuttles (even though we didn't come on them) to get Raquel's car and to get her safely to Pam's home. It was a puzzle figuring out how to get everyone home, but it was worth it because we had a great time. Plus, it's a great memory to look back on.

Throughout the next year, Damian and Marston went to San Diego's Comic-con together, did many tournaments together, and shared in their common, dorky hobbies together. Marston was a big part of our lives, and we were grateful for it.

This past year, Marston moved to Japan to get away and spend some time there. I think it's a great step for him. We will be happy to see him when he comes back, but we are ecstatic that he is somewhere that he loves and is enjoying himself.

Damian and Marston still talk frequently, and their friendship continues to grow. We look forward to seeing the man he becomes, the great writer we know he will be, and the King of a man in love he's always wanted to be.

# What is it with Playboy Models and Disneyland?

Playboy was winding down. Hef was slowly leaving the stage, and the limelight was moving onto others. But Playboy was still hanging in there. Rumors went around that Cooper was taking over in 2014. *Will Playboy last? How will it change?* These questions were on everyone's minds. Playboy had been dwindling for a while, and the parties and events were getting smaller and smaller due to money and Hef's increasing age. I was blessed to still be in an elite group of just a few left in the inner circle of the Playboy Mansion. I was waiting ever-so-watchful to see what life threw my way next. Well, that just so happened to be a friendship with Crystal. This friendship made me the first person to be Hef's guest, a friend to Crystal, and a friend to Marston. I was, definitely, in an interesting place.

That being said, in the beginning of 2014, Crystal came to me and invited me to go to Disneyland with her. I knew I had no choice but to say yes. Crystal was increasingly getting friendlier with me, and I knew that I was trapped. There were two ways to handle this:

1. I could push off her advances to be my friend, which would be rude and, inevitably, get me kicked out of the Mansion.
2. I could accept her friendship and know that my time was limited, because it seemed that Crystal couldn't keep friends around for too long.

Well, I refused to be rude, and I did like Crystal, so I accepted her friendship, thus dooming my time at the Mansion. From this point on, the idea was looming over my head that this was my last year with everyone. I didn't know how specifically, but it was clear that a friendship with Crystal would eventually lead to banishment.

On January 22, 2014, I went to Disneyland with Crystal for the first time. It started because Crystal saw that I was hosting a group trip to Disneyland, so she was inspired to host her own event. She asked me to go, and I said I would. A day before the trip, I got an email from the office stating that we would be going to Disney in a Sprinter van. We were to meet at the Mansion at 10:15am, and we would be brought back at the end of the day after watching World of Color. They said that Hef had graciously offered to cover the costs of the tickets and meals, and Caya and Crystal were taking care of the guide for the day to make the experience that much more fun.

Even though it was not necessary, I was pretty stoked to be driven to Disneyland in a Sprinter. Plus, having a tour guide was something extraordinary. It meant that you were guided around the park and taken through the exits of the rides so that you didn't have to wait in a single line. That ensured that you did not miss any ride that you wanted to do on your trip. I am told that it costs roughly $300 an hour to hire a guide (or if you are a Club 33 member, you get a certain number of guided visits a year). I definitely felt blessed at that moment.

The morning of our trip, I woke up extremely early to ensure that I'd be ready. I was told the van departed at 10:15am, so I arrived at the Mansion at 10am. When I got there, security said, "Ok. You are on the list... park your car by the garage area." This was different than what I was used to, because there was valet on the weekends, so this was my first attempt at parking at the Mansion. After forcing my car into a spot, I came in and waited in the dining room for the rest of the girls to arrive. Slowly but surely, everyone filtered in. We ordered smoothies and coffee from the kitchen (a couple of the girls ordered mojitos and put them in coffee cups so it didn't look like they were drinking at 10am), and everyone gathered into the Sprinter to depart to Disney.

There wound up being seven girls in the sprinter: Carly Lauren, Amanda Cerny, Kara Monaco, Jaslyn Ome, Crystal, Caya, and myself. Then, later in the day, Jaclyn Swedberg and Ciara Price joined us as well. Despite there only being nine girls, there were three Mansion security guards that came with us AND two Disney guides. It was crazy. We were surrounded by a swarm of people just there to help us and round us up. The security was made to look big, but it was really only necessary to keep an eye on us and to ensure that we behaved, I'm sure. Crystal seemed to be just like me on the way to Disney—incredibly excited. This was her happy place, as it was mine. (The way I liked to put it, Crystal didn't drink alcohol, and I very rarely did. Most people go out drinking to have fun. Well, Disney was our idea of fun because we were child-like people. Disney actually brought Crystal and I together and became the glue of our friendship for a long time.)

Once we arrived, we pulled into the Grand Californian Hotel. We were greeted by our Disney guides, one female and one male, both dressed in dapper button-up suits, bright red and blue checkered vests, and very clean shoes. The girl had a matching skirt, and the guy had matching pants. Our first two security guards were there with them, and our last was with us in the van. We were rounded up, and then we made our way out of the resort to our first stop: Fantasyland at Disneyland Park. We were led to the *Peter Pan* ride, where we went in through the exit to cut the line.

Throughout the day, we went from Fantasyland to Toon Town to Tomorrowland to Adventureland and all around Disneyland Park. We waited in no lines at all, and if Crystal wanted to ride a ride again, she'd just circle her finger in the air and say, "Again," and they'd let us ride again. What a day! The guides told us secrets to some rides—such as the secret to being picked as the rebel spy on the Star Tours ride—and they told us about blueprints they'd seen for future park renovations and attractions. They even helped show us many hidden Mickeys that were all over the park. (Disney Imagineers, in the creation of rides and attractions, hid little Mickey heads all over the park. It is actually fun going around and spotting them.)

Crystal showed me where several of the hidden Mickeys were. We bonded quite a bit because I knew a lot of secrets about the park that I was able to tell her about as well. She demanded that I sit with her on the *Indiana Jones* ride so she could point out the hidden Mickey ears, but we never found them—not even after riding three times in a row.

Next, we went to Disney's California Adventure Park, where we rode *Cars* multiple times. We travelled all around that park having fun, too. We even stopped at 1901, which is a special hangout for drinks and food (a lounge) for Club 33 platinum members. I was amused because they played classical versions of Disney songs and had a lot of Walt memorabilia hanging on the walls. It was a very homey place.

It wound up being such a great day, and it was so kind of Hef to treat everyone. They even covered any food expenses that we had that day. We had a good laugh during our lunch, too, because a woman in the bakery thought that Crystal, Kara, Ciara, and I were sisters. Crystal just laughed and said, "Yeah, we are!" The woman said "I can tell." We all chuckled as we walked away.

I learned a lot about who Crystal really was that day. She can be very kind, and she wants to do a lot of nice things for others. She likes to play, and, at Disney, she can do that. She can be goofy and mess with the security and have fun. She's a little obnoxious at times, but aren't we all? The more time I spent around Crystal, the more I liked her. The more I liked her, the more I began to doubt all the rumors that she was as vicious as people made her out to be. But, I knew I shouldn't put my guard down. She could, actually, be very nice if she liked you. The problem was that when you got on her bad side, that was it. She had no tolerance for you at all.

Hef had reserved the very front of Paradise Pier for us to watch The World of Color at the end of our day. We had benches reserved for us to watch the show. As the show began, Crystal stood up to get a better view of the waterworks. There was a woman who had stopped to see the show behind us who said, "Excuse me, you need to sit down" in a very commanding tone. With that comment, Crystal freaked out. "We paid to be here!"

"*Se hables ingles*?" someone else said to her from behind as she tried to ignore the rude comments, and, with that last one, she snapped. She grabbed security and made them get Disneyland security to stand with us.

She did have a right to get upset; after all, they did pay a lot of money to have those spots, and the people behind her could have easily moved, as they did not have a specific spot to watch the show. They were just moseying by on the walkway behind our seats. But it escalated because the guys behind us said, "I'm sure they paid for the spots with the money from the strip club." The nasty remarks continued. As a result, Disneyland security came, and they all ran away very fast.

All in all, I had a great day bonding with all of these girls. Plus, I discovered that Crystal was a great host. She took turns sitting with everyone on the rides. She went back and forth on who she sat with and talked to everyone over the course of the day. We bonded and wound up really getting along. I liked the whole group. And, at the end of the day, Crystal said, "I'm really glad that I brought you all. This was the best group by far."

When we were leaving, someone sent Crystal a picture of a "Ghost Bunny" that was taken at the Mansion that actually looked really disturbing. She freaked out, and we spent the evening talking about how horrifying the house was and how it had to be haunted. With that ghost story, our miraculous adventure at Disney had ended.

The following day, I was at work when I received an email from Barbara at the Playboy Mansion office. She said that I was invited to watch *Cinderella* with Crystal that night at the Mansion—Crystal wanted to invite all the girls who went to Disneyland to watch *Cinderella*. It was very sweet. I took a few hours off of work to come in and watch it. Again, I drove up, parked my car, and went in just before the movie. It was my first Thursday movie night, and it wouldn't be my last.

My mind began to wander after Crystal invited a couple of us to sit with her during the movie. The truth of the matter was as follows: it's not easy being the odd man out of the group. Amongst all of my friends in this situation (give or take one or two), I was the only one who wasn't a Playmate. Pam and Raquel would run off together at times to work certain jobs, and I couldn't go work it because I wasn't a Playmate. I would see my friends all doing great things together, and I couldn't be there. Crystal was so good about not treating me like I was different. I'm sure it was because she couldn't do promotions herself, as the mistress of the Mansion, so she treated me no differently than anyone else, and I loved that. I began to trust her completely, as Crystal did her best to never make me feel left out. That may have been a bad judgment call on my part, but I did enjoy my time with her.

In the end of May, Marston graduated from his private college in Orange County. He asked Damian and me to be there. The plan was, after the event, we were going to meet our guide at Disneyland to participate in a guided tour (just like what I had done with Crystal). We sat through rain sprinkles during his entire ceremony, but by the time the graduation was over, the rain was done. We went to Disneyland and got there an hour early, so we ate a nice meal at the Grand California Hotel. Once we met our guide, we did everything we would want to do at Disneyland in six hours, as the guide had us cutting all the lines for every ride. For *Indiana Jones,* we rode three times in a row. For Space Mountain, we rode twice. We even got our own elevator on the Haunted Mansion, and there were only six of us.

It was a great day. Our guide, Justin, was really quiet at first. We had to open him up. I was asking him a lot of silly questions to make him comfortable with us. By the end, he seemed to realize that we were a pretty cool group, and he lightened up. He told us about Disneyland jail and that it was really just a waiting-room behind the Main Street Opera House. Justin also gave me a great idea for my birthday, as it was just two weeks away at this point.

There are guided Disneyland tours offered to Disney pass holders that have different purposes. They are only $80 or less, and they last about three hours. These tours take you around and give you specific information about the park. So, for my birthday through Justin's recommendation, we did the "Walk in Walt's Disneyland Footsteps" tour, and it was amazing. Plus, I can say, Raquel made my birthday extra special that year.

As I had mentioned, Raquel had made her way into becoming my best friend. That being said, her other best friend had the same birthday as me. She was in Tijuana the night before for her other best friend's birthday. She left early in the morning to come meet me at Disneyland for my celebration. Pamela came with me pretty early, and we met Raquel before the tour outside of the park. Raquel surprised me with shirts that she had made. Mine said "It's my BDay," and Raquel and Pamela's said, "Happy BDay Mal!" I was so touched. She had gone out of her way to have surprise shirts made for me. Then, because Pamela couldn't afford it, Raquel paid for her tour to be sure we could do this special event.

The tour was a little boring. We went around to each area of the park, learning the history. Some of it was cool, but other sections of the journey weren't as interesting. We heard Walt's Opening Day speech over our audio equipment, and we got to cut the line to ride *Peter Pan* and *The Enchanted Tiki Room*.

The best part of the tour was at the end. It was what I was waiting for the whole time. As we made our way back to the tour guide station, we gathered for the main event. We divided into groups and took turns going into Walt's Apartment for the end of the tour. You see, Walt Disney had an apartment that he would stay in above the Firehouse on

Main Street within Disneyland Park. This was the real reason I wanted to do the tour. I will explain:

Crystal's birthday was a little over a month before my own. Because she got me into Club 33 the year before, I wanted to make it up to her. I got her a Thomas Kinkade *Little Mermaid* Disney print for her birthday. It was framed, and she said she loved it. I gave it to her at dinner one night, and she told me that she was going to hang it over her bed. Pamela was with me on this day, so Crystal invited the two of us to go to Disney with her that Wednesday. She said we'd do a guided trip, and that we should invite whoever we wanted. She also invited us on a tour of Walt's apartment at this time. (Apparently, Club 33 members can schedule visits to Walt's Apartment.)

Now, my opinion of Crystal is that she's great at manipulating. I think this is because she fully believes something when she says it, but then she changes her mind later, after having forgotten the first thing she said. Because she's so spontaneous, she truly means what she says in the heat of the moment, so it isn't really a lie. However, she will change her mind, frequently. That being said, we didn't hear from her until the day before we were supposed to go to Disney. Pamela asked her, on the Tuesday before we were going, if she still wanted to go. Crystal replied, "Sorry, I can't anymore. I'm filming something tomorrow." The following day, we saw on Facebook that she had a birthday brunch, and she didn't invite us to it. I thought it was funny because I expected nothing less. When I texted Crystal that we were still up for the Walt's apartment tour, she said, "Oh, I really can't bring many people" and dismissed the idea for good. Having something I really wanted dangled in my face and then having it snatched away lit a fire under me. Now I had to go and see Walt's Apartment. So when I was at Disney with Justin, I asked him about the apartment. He said, "You either have to be a Club 33 member or take the 'Walk in Walt's Footsteps Tour' to see the apartment." When I told Raquel about it, she made the tour happen for my birthday.

Before I transition further into my birthday, I do want to make a comment about the whole Crystal issue. She texted me many months later and explained this situation to me. She told me that she wished she had gone with me to Disneyland that day instead of trying to make everyone happy. She said she had to film her dance submission for *Dancing with the Stars* that day, but Alison threw a surprise party for her last minute, after her audition tape appointment. She said it was an awkward affair where she wasn't even very close with the girls that Alison invited. She said no one would pay for their food, and it put her in an odd place where she felt obligated to pay for everyone. She told me that she wished she could take it back and go to Disney with me. Whether or not that was fully true, I had an amazing time on my birthday.

It was a great accomplishment for me when we went to Walt's Apartment. The tour guide took us through a gate behind-the-scenes to the right of the Firehouse on Main Street. Once backstage, we made an immediate left up a pair of metal stairs. They moved in a square shape, around and up, until we reached a platform. The platform was the entrance into Walt's Apartment. The tour guide stopped and said, "Hey birthday girl, why don't you ring the doorbell?"

With that, I got to ring Walt's doorbell three times for good luck. It was an old crank doorbell that looked almost like a deadbolt. I turned it three times to the right, and the bell echoed in the apartment. Then, he opened up the door, and we all stepped inside. Once inside Walt's apartment, we were blown away. It was silent and very homey inside. To the left was an old-fashioned coat rack for us to hang our things on. I hung my wallet on there. To the right was a coat closet. When walking in, you went a few feet past these two things and into the main apartment (a tiny, 500 square-foot room). Aside from the bathroom and the patio, that was the entire apartment. It was a rectangular room with a couch ending both of the smaller walls. Looking straight ahead at Main Street, there was a window and a small bed table. The table had a light on it, which was always lit in honor of Walt. When he was on the premises, he would have that lit so employees knew he was there. Now, it is eternally lit in his honor, as he is always at Disneyland.

There was a red couch to the left and to the right of the room. The carpet itself was also a velvety red. The apartment seemed very old with Victorian style décor, and there were also chairs in the corners around the couches. The couches were fold-out beds where Walt and Lillian would sleep when they stayed on the premises. Walt had the left side, and Lillian had the right. Behind us, on the opposing wall to Main Street, was Walt's kitchen. It was a tiny space that could be closed off by wicker doors (like a closet). We got to see Walt's plates, cups, and kitchenware in there. It was floral and beautiful. Also, there were sets that said "Tom and Jerry," notating a famous drink of the time period. As far as cooking, there was a grilled cheese press in there, as Walt liked to have a grilled cheese every day. Next to the kitchen sat a beautiful stand-up mirror with Disneyland knick-knacks from the 60s on it. Some of them still had price tags from Disneyland on them. There was also an old music-box machine that played classical music. Up the back of the apartment, across the kitchen and away from the entrance, were a few steps that went up and led to the patio. To the right of the patio was the bathroom. The bathroom was the only "modern" part of the apartment. It was a very 60s looking bathroom with four shower heads in the shower. For some reason that man had four shower heads hooked up and working in his shower!

This vision of Walt's apartment was sketched in my head for the rest of the night. After celebrating at Disneyland, we went to sleep over at Pam's apartment. Raquel gave me an amazing birthday gift that her mother made. It was a hand-made towel that had my name and a photo of Elsa from *Frozen* on it. It was amazing. She wasn't the only one that got me a great gift. Crystal had gotten me a whole bag of things from Hot Topic that were Disney related. There was a Cinderella keychain, two charms (one *Rapunzel* and the other *Lady and the Tramp*), a *Frozen* shirt, and *Frozen* socks that she handed to me in a bag a few days later. Then, Crystal told me my big present hadn't arrived yet. She ordered me a special-made wallet that had a scene from *Frozen* on it. The inside of the wallet was designed with a map of Disneyland. It was another very thoughtful gift. With that it seemed, just like many other girls in the Playboy World, I was fully submerged into the Disneyland lifestyle.

# Taken In

Once you are taken in by the Hefner family, apparently you are pulled in all around. At least that's what happened with me. For the remainder of the year, Crystal began texting me almost every day. It would be quick comments some days and long conversations on others. She would text me silly nothings or show me cute *Frozen* pictures from Instagram. Then, on July 16th, 2014, she asked me to go with her and see the new Club 33 before it opened (as it had been under renovations for six months and was completely remodeled). It officially re-opened for reservations on July 18th, but as a member Crystal got to see it two days early. Of course, I said yes.

I met Crystal that day thinking it would be a few of us girls going together. Little did I know, it wound up being just the two of us. (This idea made me nervous, as I had never spent any real one-on-one time with her before.) We met at the Mansion very early in the morning and drove in her Tesla over to Disneyland. We got to do a full tour of the new Club 33 area, and we were the first group ever to see it. It was an amazing experience. The only part that was the same from the previous club design was the main dining hall. Everything else was expanded off the back side of the premises. We went into the new club through what used to be a gift shop. It was a tiny room now used just as a reception area.

Once we arrived at the club, we rang the doorbell, and they let us in through that reception area and into a courtyard (what used to be the Court of Angels). There was a fountain in the middle of the courtyard with chairs around it. The new gates that sealed off the court were beautiful with floral designs on them, and the stairs up to the patio and the elevator they put in were painted blue. We walked up each winding step to the balcony where the entrance to the club was now located. Each step had a pretty drooping flower light on it guiding our way up. The phone booth from the old Club 33 was there as well, hiding in a corner on the balcony upstairs before the entrance, as were the restrooms.

The restrooms at the new club were almost humorous. The men's bathroom was dark blue with horses placed everywhere. There was a bookshelf to accent the style as well. It was pretty much screaming the word, "STAG!" The women's room was bright pink with a nice, fluffy couch. It was too pretty for its own good. The wicker toilets from the old club design, however, were gone.

Once you made it into the entrance of the new club, you could head in one of two directions. To the left, you could walk through the wine cellar where wine was literally covering all sides of the walls around you. That path led to a jazz club. In the booths at the entranceway to the jazz club, there was amazing stained-glass art with lights shining from behind the pieces, making them glow, and many gorgeous photos of the bayou. The jazz club had a beautiful bar to the right of the entrance, lounge chairs everywhere, and a piano that could channel any live concert in the world. It was very homey and made to look similar to the jazz club from the *Princess and the Frog*. Looking out of the window, I could tell that it was over the French Market restaurant across from the Haunted Mansion and the Train Station. I found out that this section was for members only and members with their guests. (If a member makes a reservation for you, you can't go there without them).

If you traveled to the right of the main Club 33 entrance, that path took you down a long set of hallways that connected to the main dining room. The main dining room now had black and white floors instead of the wooden ones it used to have. They got rid of the fireplace and replaced it with a large, open window. This room now had a much more modern feel to it.

The old Trophy room and the old club entrance, however, were no more. The kitchen had been expanded to that area, but the new entrance and areas were too beautiful for you to miss the trophy room.

Crystal and I spent the time around our tour talking about anything and everything. She really opened up to me that day about the friends that she used to have and how she lost them. At least, I thought that she had opened up to me. From what I know about her now, I believe that she makes up a fake version of something that happens and convinces herself that it is true. This ensures that she is the victim in any situation, which is exactly where she wants to be.

Regardless, we spoke about how she had a falling out with Anna Sophia Berglund and with Ashley Matthau, who were people she, at one time, considered to be her best friends. She really made me believe that she got a lot of unnecessary flak from people that didn't understand her. She said that a lot of girls get thrown off the list at the Playboy Mansion for not coming enough or because they don't have enough involvement with the company to keep getting the free food and drinks. From what she described to me, I do feel that Crystal may have been oblivious to some of this, and she did get a lot of hate that she didn't deserve from people. A lot of it, though, I'm sure she did deserve. She wasn't an angel, but I didn't believe that she was a devil either.

The more we spoke, the more I noticed that she seemed to come off almost high, or at least very flighty all the time. I talked to her about the group trip to Disney that we had taken together, and she didn't remember that it happened, despite the event occurring less than six months prior to the day I was describing. I had to lay out every detail of the trip for her before she remembered.

Then, we went to the Disney Gallery, which was turned into an amazing display of Club 33 merchandise. As we were being shown all of the new goodies, a scary thought sunk into my brain—I was a friend of

Crystal's. I had always been afraid to be her friend, but now it didn't seem so bad. In fact, I enjoyed being Crystal's friend. She was funny, spontaneous, and she loved Disney like I did. After spending the day together, she began inviting me to every special Thursday screening they had at the Mansion since it was her night and she got to pick the movies. The guard I had up for so long seemed to drop around her, and I was happy to be in her inner circle.

Not to mention, the model signings at Bench Warmer had me mingling and interacting with a lot of the new Playmates as they were coming in to sign, so, whichever girls I didn't meet that the Mansion, I met at the Bench Warmer penthouse. Many of them were really fun, and we developed friendships of our own. I really was taken in, and every aspect of my life seemed to revolve around Playboy. Aside from my auditioning and Indie film work with Damian, everything else seemed to be clouded by the bunny. Unfortunately, there were girls, such as Alicia, who began getting jealous of my involvement with Playboy on such a deep level. I didn't blame her, because she did get me invited up in the first place, but Alicia felt as if I was ignoring her for my friendships with Pamela, Raquel, and Marston. She felt that because she wasn't a Playmate or a Hefner, she wasn't important to me. The truth was that Alicia and I were not compatible friends. It had nothing to do with her title or anything of the sort, but she didn't see it that way. She confronted me about it one day, and I tried to explain it the best I could. We discussed the situation, and I told her that I would love to hang out with her and get coffee, but she liked to party, and I did not. I made it clear that I didn't want to be going out in a club or bar-like environment much anymore. She told me we worked it out, but I didn't think that was truly the case.

The closer that I got to Crystal and all the girls and the closer that Damian got to Marston, the more I was around the Playboy environment almost every day. As a result, everyone thought that I was a Playmate. I wasn't, but everyone just assumed that I was. The butlers introduced me to new girls as "one of the Playmates" on a weekly basis. When I corrected them, they seemed to not hear me. Everyone just assumed without asking. All of the girls were my friends and treated me like a Playmate, so I guess that it didn't necessarily matter. I got so tired of trying to correct everyone that it was easier to just let people think that I was one.

And, again, the more time I spent with Crystal, the more she continued to open up to me. She began to trust me with truths that she didn't tell most people. In fact, she told me why she left Hef at the altar, which was fascinating to me since I was there through all of that fiasco. She told me that Hef and her had been fighting frequently about the wedding and how it was going to be broadcasted everywhere. She was no longer happy because she couldn't go a day without fighting with him. She said that there was one final fight that they had, and she said that she had nothing else to do at that moment then to leave to go and get some air. Hef called to security and said, "If Crystal tries to leave, detain her." She told me that, at that moment, she knew that she was a prisoner. How many people cannot leave their own house after a fight to get some air? She didn't want to be stuck like that, so she knew it was better for her sanity to leave. I couldn't believe it, but I actually understood why Crystal chose to leave Hef at the altar the way that she did.

Reflecting back on this time, I was extremely happy with Crystal, Hef, Marston, and everything I had going for me at the Playboy Mansion. But, as I mentioned before, I went into my friendship with Crystal knowing that it would be short-lived, and that experience lived up to my expectations. A very trying period of time was about to take over my world, and I wasn't really ready for it.

# And Then Everything I Knew Changed

Like all good things, I knew that my time at the Mansion had to end. I just didn't realize that it would happen so unexpectedly. On Friday

August 15th, 2014, the day before Midsummers, I got an email from Joyce. It was a generic group email addressing "Ladies," but it was sent as a blind CC, so I have no idea how many people it really went to. It was quick and simple, and it told me that my FITS privileges had ended "for now." I didn't quite understand what that meant. I started out as a Friday guest, so I didn't really care if my Sunday privileges were cut if I could still go Thursday and Friday. After all, FITS referred to our time at the Mansion on Sundays. So, I emailed Joyce asking what this meant. I had to wait the entire weekend to hear. By the time that Joyce had replied, my stomach was burning with anxiety. Come Monday, I received an email from Joyce saying, "This ends your Thursdays, Fridays, and Saturdays, too."

Just like that, everything I knew changed.

I should have seen it coming. Months before, Joel and Alison had been "temporarily taken off the list" when they had a disagreement with someone. They had to apologize to come back up, and they came back up with a lot more rules on them. If they weren't safe, no one was safe. I should have seen that as an omen of what was to come.

For the first time in my life, I felt severely flawed. Was this my fault? I really felt ancient, and I was only 26. I felt like I was in *The House Bunny*. I was numb. I wanted to cry and get it out...but I couldn't. I couldn't feel that sad, and I couldn't cry it out as much as I wanted to. It was a life-changing event. I had been at the Mansion for four years, and I couldn't feel anything about this. My husband was worried about me. He reached out consistently, and all I could think to say was this: "I'm okay. I mean, I'm sad, but I'm okay. Things happen for a reason, and I feel like I've gotten what I needed out of this experience and left with great things like my friendships with Raquel, Pamela, and Marston. It's not like I was banned; I'm just cut for now. I'm sure I'd be ok to come up now and then, and I am still on the party list. It just sounds like they are cutting girls who have been around for a while. Yeah, I wish it didn't come out of nowhere, but it's ok. I can deal with it."

Raquel seemed to be more upset than I was, and she felt lost for me. I didn't know how to feel or what to do. I wasn't sad like I thought I would be, nor did I really feel anything. I guess I was lost, but I felt fine. At Midsummers Crystal asked me, "Am I going to see you tomorrow?"

I replied, "No, I can't come Sundays anymore."

I felt that she might stop talking to me, but she didn't. She texted me the following day like normal. Once I got the notice that everything was cut, I texted her the following day, "Hey! I just heard back from Joyce today, and it looks like I'm cut from everything—including Thursdays and Fridays. So, I won't really be around anymore. I don't want that to mean we don't see each other, though! I've really enjoyed when we spent time together. Maybe we can do Disney one morning coming up or get lunch or something one day."

She replied, "Yeah, Disney for sure and hangs. I don't see much of people when they come here anyways, since I'm usually glued to my phone and to Hef." After that point, she ignored the fact that I was banned. She just never mentioned that I couldn't go up. (Knowing what I know now, I definitely should have been suspicious of this. I was trying too hard to give Crystal the benefit of the doubt, as I am a forgiving and slightly naïve person.) She texted me every now and then like she usually did, and I was surprised. Perhaps Crystal really wasn't going to push me aside because I couldn't go up anymore? She told me before that she hated that people blamed her once they got cut from the list, so I made sure to let her know I was okay with her and did not blame her—even though I knew that she had the power to fix it. I also knew that she wouldn't. From what I knew about Crystal, I assumed that she wouldn't reach out for others and put herself on the line, but I was okay with that. As long as she was still talking to me, it was okay. But, on my more solemn days, it did cross my mind that she may have been toying with me and testing how strong our friendship was or if we were really friends at all. Or, just maybe, I did something to bother her, and she was hiding the truth from me?

Finally, it hit me. A week or so later, I had stayed up all night working. At the end of the night, I sent the following to Joel and Alison in my delirious state, as I realized that I hadn't told them, "Hey guys! Just wanted to reach out and say that we should do lunch or something soon. I have been cut from weekends at the Mansion, so I won't be seeing you as much anymore, but I don't want that to mean we lose touch. I'll probably be less in the loop so please keep me updated about the pub crawls, garden bar events, and usual nights out as Damian and I would love to attend, as always. And hopefully we can do lunch some time coming up! Talk to you soon."

I woke up just a few hours later to use the restroom, and both Joel and Alison had already replied to me. Joel said, "Malorie, my love, you and Damian will always be in our loop... We love and adore you and Damian. Don't let this bum you out. I hope to see you very soon. Much love, Joel (and Alison)."

Then, Alison followed up with this, "Joel just told me this, and I am bummed. I love you guys. So YES we will stay in touch. Garden Bar is always open to you guys. Lunch or dinner is always open, too. You are a big part of our lives, and you are on the permanent pub crawl list. At some point it will all come to an end, and we all will still be friends and see each other a lot. So sorry. My love to you and Damian. Come by any time. Our door is always open."

I told them more or less what I had told Damian and Raquel, "Aaaaw, thanks for all the love and support. You guys are amazing, and we love you guys, too. I'm actually very fine with everything. There's so much I gained from my experiences at the Mansion, like great friendships with you two, Raquel, Pamela, Marston, and Crystal. None of these things are changing, and I will still be seeing everyone around. Yes! I'll shoot you a call next week, Alison, as I will be around. You guys are amazing! See you soon and looking forward to the next pub crawl, too!"

Joel and Alison's kind, hippy love made me emotional about my banishment for the first time. And, for the first time after being kicked out, I cried. Yet, at the same time, I was very conflicted. Everyone was so overwhelmed. They were treating the situation like it was so tragic and dire. They kept telling me how horrible it was for me that I couldn't go back, but I didn't really feel that way. Sure, it was a life-changing event, but it wasn't the end of the world. I had been getting tired of the Mansion, and my visits were less and less frequent. I did not need the Mansion to validate myself. There were so many wonderful things I had gotten out of it since my first visit years before, and I had so many great experiences there. As I mentioned above, I still had friendships with Raquel, Pamela, Joel and Alison, Marston, and (dare I say it) Crystal. Crystal was still texting me, so not much had changed. Plus, I had this odd feeling that my involvement with the Mansion wasn't over. I didn't know if it was because the invitation would re-open to me or maybe just because my friends were still with me, and the only thing I lost was a place to hang out. Whatever it was, I really did not feel that my involvement with Playboy was over, but if it was, my overall experience there left me with a feeling of happiness. So, what was there to feel bad about? After all, what you took from the Mansion was all based on your own state of mind. If I had only positive experiences there, I could always look back on it with happiness. That was what I had intended to do.

Shortly after this happened, at a house-warming party for Raquel I got some very real advice from a friend. My anonymous friend said, "Malorie, as your friend, I want to be completely honest with you. The only people who can make changes to the list are Crystal and Hef. Crystal, generally, knocks off girls that she doesn't like, and that's it. It's strange in your case though, because she's still talking to you. Maybe Hef said something about you being cute or made a comment about you that made Crystal uncomfortable? So, maybe she wants you for herself and not for Hef or anyone else around."

It hurt hearing that Crystal had to have cut me, but it was something that I had always known deep down. I felt as if she was testing me, and

I still didn't quite understand why. What I was told made a lot of sense...but there had to be something I was missing. Lucky for me, I would, eventually, find out what had happened.

# A Second Chance

After a few weeks of being away from the Mansion, Crystal began texting me less and less. I worried a bit but decided the best thing to do was to move on and not let her get to me. At the beginning of October, I reached out to her about doing a "Happy Haunts" tour of Disneyland (because she had told me a few months prior that she wanted to do it). Sure enough, she said that she wanted to go. Being in the position that I was in, I offered to get the tickets for the tour because I knew it would be a nice gesture, and I wanted to do something nice for Crystal, who had done a lot for me in the past. So, I set up our Happy Haunts tour for October 20th, 2014. Since it was on a Monday, Crystal said that she was allowed to be out until 9pm, rather than the normal 5pm curfew for movie nights. Because of this, we signed up for the 4:45pm tour and planned on getting to Disney early to experience the day.

After setting up our trip, Crystal began texting me more and more. Then, two weeks before, I was shocked to find an invite to Crystal's Thursday movie night in my email. I had been invited back up to the Mansion again! Sure, it was only for one night, but it was something. It was nostalgic going back up. Upon going back to the Mansion for the first time in months, it was easy to see how the dynamic of my invitation had changed. I was going as Crystal's friend now. I was invited to her night only, and I was no longer one of Hef's regular guests. Crystal seemed to make this clear to me without ever having to say anything. She came down, spotted me, acted surprised, and said she was so excited to see me. She talked with me across the table at dinner, and then she asked me to sit on Hef's couch with her and Hef during the movie. This was a big deal. The spots on the couch next to Hef were always for the girlfriends, and, since he was married, Crystal occasionally invited friends to sit there with her. We went in, sat on the couch, and lifted our feet up on to the footstools. Hef sat on the far left (like always), Crystal was in the middle, and I was on the far right. She spent the movie (*Labyrinth*) whispering funny comments to me about David Bowie's package. Hef would lean over and say something cute to her every now and then or ask her something like, "What was your favorite age? Mine was high school." At one point, in the middle of the movie, she turned to me and asked if I wanted to order food. I told her that I was fine. She said, "Well, split a grilled cheese with me?" I agreed. We watched the movie, ate our grilled cheese, and Charlie even jumped up on my lap and cuddled with me. She told me how excited she was for the 20th, and I was getting excited for it too.

It wasn't until the 20th that I saw her again, as I wasn't invited to the next movie night. (Could it have been an accident that I was invited to that one? She did look pretty surprised to see me.) That morning of the 20th, I pulled up into the Mansion driveway at 11:30am and parked in the loop. I waited for Crystal for about five minutes in the dining room until she came down. She gave me a big hug and acted so happy to see me. She was dressed in an Ariel shirt and I was dressed in an Elsa shirt, so that was a fun gesture, as they were our favorite characters. We went in her car, once again, to Disneyland.

On the way to the park, we began talking, and it felt like everything was okay again. In person, Crystal always seemed to make me feel like we were closer than we actually were. She was so fun and easy to talk to. When it was just the two of us, we would talk about anything and everything. On this particular day, we talked about past experiences, people, and events until we got to Disneyland. I wanted to bring up what I had heard. In my mind I had a whole dialogue going on. *Should I address the fact that I know she kicked me out? She'll never be honest about it.* I couldn't muster up the courage to talk about the subject. I enjoyed our time together, and we were still hanging out, so I decided it was best to not bring up the subject. I didn't want to cause any more issues.

Once we got there, we took advantage of the free valet parking at the Grand California Hotel that she got as a Club 33 member. She was asking me about Alicia as we pulled up, and I mentioned to her that Alicia originally came up because she was seeing Morgan. Crystal freaked out and belted a huge laugh! She had no idea. As she contained herself to get out of the car and go to California Adventure to start the day, she told me to hold up because she needed to take her vitamins. She opened a container of many, many vitamins. She was telling me what each one was until she got to one pill and said, "And this one makes my poop not smell." Apparently, according to what she told me that day, she took vitamins to keep her poop and farts from smelling, so she wouldn't ever embarrass herself in public.

After the shock of hearing about that pill wore off, we decided to get lunch at the bread bowl place in California Adventure. Upon arriving, we saw a line of people coming out of the store. Crystal was not impressed with the line, so she suggested that we go to 1901 for lunch instead. 1901 was the Club 33-equivalent lounge at California Adventure that only Club 33 members with platinum membership levels were allowed to go to. It was the nice place with pictures of Walt all over that I had mentioned visiting on our group trip. Crystal was nice enough to cover lunch because I paid for the trip. It was at this point that I discovered that she had a very healthy appetite. We both ordered the grilled cheese with tomato soup, but she also got us two small platters to share. When we went to leave, she asked if I wanted a cake pop to go. I told her that I was too full, but she insisted, so we each ate a cake pop on the way out. They melted quickly, and we went into a boutique to get her shoes, so they were getting everywhere in the store. We laughed and went outside to get rid of them before they destroyed anything.

Crystal bought a pair of shoes at the DCA boutique so she would be more comfortable, as she had come in wedges. On our way over to

Disneyland Park from California Adventure, she told me that she felt that Playboy was going downhill. I agreed that with Playboy Plus happening, Playboy got a really bad name. We both agreed that the company was cleaning up the mess that Playboy Plus had made for them, and it was a pretty successful cleanup. I made a joke and said, "Well, you know it's bad when Russell gets a promotion."

With that, we made it into Disneyland and began heading down towards Adventureland. Crystal's new shoes were not working for her, so we went back into a boutique at Disneyland. She got another pair of shoes that were much more comfortable. The second pair of shoes wound up being the charm. Her Club 33 membership, at this time, allowed her to have six immediate Fast Passes a day. So, she could put in for a Fast Pass, and it would come out with the current time on it. We used one to get immediately onto *Indiana Jones*. We requested the back and had a great ride on it. As we road, we were discussing my marriage; she was excited to find that both of us had our wedding anniversaries within the same week and a half.

We then went to Splash Mountain and got lucky because we got seats 5 and 6 (which are the seats on the back of the boat where you get the least wet). Unfortunately, Crystal wanted the front and asked if we could wait for the next boat to get the front. So, we waited for the next boat. Crystal took the front seat, and I took the second. By the time we got off of Splash Mountain, we were soaking wet. Waves of water came right over the front of the boat and into my lap. Crystal ducked and got her hair and her back soaked. We got off the boats looking like we showered at Disneyland.

At that point, we made our way back to the tour gardens to start our event. We got situated, got special name tags, and got ear pieces to hear the tour better. It started off down Main Street, where they told us simple facts about Halloween and the pumpkins decorating Disneyland. Then, we went to the Haunted Mansion where we were followed out by a "hitchhiking ghost" named Master Gracey. Master Gracey is the head of the Haunted Mansion, who told us his tragic story. Then, we went to Big Thunder Mountain where we learned a few new secrets about that ride, too. Finally, we made our way down to Tomorrowland to Ride Space Mountain. It was a great treat because we cut the lines for all of these rides, as it was a tour, and these were rides that generally had very long waits. Next, we went down to the alley by the Starbucks where we trick or treated for special treats. We got a marshmallow pumpkin, a pumpkin cookie, and a special sample cup of Halloween-time Starbucks drinks.

As the tour ended, we got a special pin that was shaped like the key to the Haunted Mansion. Our ghost host left us and said that we could always find him at the Haunted Mansion, and then we heard gun shots as he disappeared backstage. Perhaps that was some dark Disney humor? After that, Crystal claimed that she was ready to go back for all the other Disneyland tours and requested that we try them all together.

The evening after the tour, I reflected back on the day, and I remembered that Crystal had dropped a lot of clues about my pulled invitation from the Mansion. Throughout the day, with us talking about people in our lives, Crystal laid down little hints about Alicia that led me to believe that she was the reason I got kicked out of the Mansion. How ironic would it be if Alicia, the girl that got me into the Mansion, had gotten me kicked out?

I reviewed the day in my mind: First, as we were arriving, Crystal asked me what I thought of Alicia. As I had mentioned before, I told her that Alicia started coming around because she was dating Morgan. I told her that Alicia was cool. I liked her, but we weren't really close. I told her that Alicia got mad at me for a while for not inviting her out. She felt that we had to be friends, but I only wanted to spend time with her at the Mansion. The truth was, I could never really be close to Alicia because we had different ideas of fun. Sure, she was great to hang out with at the Mansion, but I didn't want to go out to the club with her because I hated clubbing. Crystal said, "I know. Alicia said that you were a user and didn't care about her. She said you just wanted to hang out with Playmates and wouldn't give anyone else the time of day." It hurt that Alicia would say that to Crystal. I knew she felt that way, as we had discussed it. She was mad at me, but how dare she say something so untrue to Crystal.

I turned to Crystal and said, "You know what, her thinking that says something about her. I don't see people as Playmate or not a Playmate. I see people for who they are. I don't see labels like that, and, clearly, Alicia does." I took a second to soak it all in and continued, "You know, Crystal, I feel bad about Alicia. She always wanted to hang out, and I was just too busy. Then, when it came down to it, we just were not compatible. She likes to party and drink, and I don't drink. I'm married. I like to curl up in bed and watch movies. We just weren't right as friends." I continued to explain that it took me years in LA to get true friends at all, as I am very stand-offish. I explained that I've always been quiet and kept to myself, and I am just getting comfortable with people. Alicia and I just didn't fit together, and when I wouldn't go out drinking with her, she got mad at me. Crystal got that. She told me that if I didn't feel comfortable with someone or compatible with them, then it definitely wasn't worth the trouble.

Later on, Crystal asked me if I ever tested for Playmate. I told her that I hadn't. Crystal replied, "Alicia said you tested."

I responded very clearly, "Alicia doesn't know what she's talking about."

Finally, at the end of the night, Crystal brought up that Alicia had asked if we were hanging out. Now, when she said that, I began putting the pieces together. I formed my own conspiracy theory in my head. First—I have to say that I don't know if Crystal was talking to Alicia directly or if Alicia told Caya (because they were best friends), and Caya told Crystal (because they were best friends). That last option seemed much more plausible. Regardless of whether or not it was direct, I wasn't happy about it. Here's what I pieced together: Alicia, or Caya, having seen that Crystal and I spent time together in July at Club 33, went to Crystal and asked if we spent time together. This frustrated Alicia, as she has always tried to be my friend, but it never worked out. So then she had to tell Crystal not to trust me because she thought that I was a user and only wanted to hang out with Playmates and people I could get stuff out of. Clearly, in her head, I was just trying to be a Playmate, as she was telling people that I was testing. So, Crystal knew she enjoyed spending time with me, but she got scared by what Alicia said. After all, it seemed that Crystal had a very hard time trusting people (I don't blame her). We finally got close and Alicia made her doubt me entirely. So, I got kicked out of the Mansion, but she continued to talk to me because she liked me, and she knew that we had fun together.

When I paid for her Happy Haunts tour and offered it to her, she realized that I wasn't a user if I was offering to pay for her. So, she gave me another chance. Thank God she did, as I was able to tell her my side of this silly story. She completely understood my side, and I was so grateful that I had this opportunity to explain myself about Alicia and fix my relationship with Crystal.

Of course, all of what I just said was, at this time, a conspiracy theory circling in my mind. I had no proof other than hints that Crystal dropped, but she had given me a strong cause to let my mind start to believe this. How could she make me act so crazy? Perhaps it was because Alicia was a sore spot for me. From what I actually understood later about what had happened, my hunch did have a lot of truth to it. Both Alicia and Caya were, in fact, in Crystal's ear about me while we were hanging out. I had tried very hard to get along with Alicia because we had some great times at the Mansion together, but, after some time, it was clear that Alicia and I shouldn't hang out outside of the Mansion because we had nothing else in common. I felt bad, as she continually got mad that I wouldn't hang out with her, but I made other friends that I got along with. Because of this, I got her a modeling job working with Bench Warmer, which she desperately wanted, and then we would see each other at Bench Warmer from time to time, too. She still must not have cared for me, even after that. I guess there was nothing I could do to appease Alicia.

I began to get mad at myself for caring so much. Why was I still hanging out with Crystal after she banned me from her home? Why did it matter what she or Alicia thought of me? For some reason I was just caught up in everything again. I don't know why I didn't just drop everything there. I don't know why I continued to see these people that were playing games with me. I don't know what motivated me to want to continue to be accepted by them, but I did keep going along for the ride.

# A False Sense of Security

Two days after our Disney tour, as Crystal and I planned, I woke up and made her my "Woman Crush Wednesday" on Instagram. I put up a photo of her and posted, "My #wcw is the gorgeous @crystalhefner. This woman can accomplish anything she sets her mind to. She is beautiful on the inside and out." Next thing I know, Crystal starts liking different photos that I posted from a long time ago (clearly going through my photos all the way back to the beginning). She liked the wallet photo I posted from when I got her gift and the photo I took years ago under her and Hef's wedding arch. I thought, *she must be looking for a photo to post for my Woman Crush Wednesday, as she told me she was going to post me.*

As if on cue, that minute she posted me on her Instagram to her (at the time) 379,000 followers saying, "My #wcw is my beautiful Disney partner in crime @maloriemackey." It was sweet. I was immediately excited that Crystal finally posted me. But, as I was learning, like all things with Crystal, there is always a catch or something to rain on your parade. Two hours after posting it, she took it down. I had to wonder... *Did someone give her a hard time for posting that? Was it Alicia? Was she closer to Alicia than I thought? Did she do that as a charity to me? Maybe she doesn't like me as much and had to take it down right away?* Of course, nothing was ever easy with her. I started to ask myself, "Is it worth it being friends with Crystal? Is the stress that comes with her friendship worth my constant anxiety?"

I got home that evening and texted Crystal. I told her that I was going to send her my check for the Splash Mountain Club 33 event we were going to together. We were planning to attend this in a couple of weeks, and it was not cheap. I needed to send her my half of the event payment. She replied and told me not to worry about it. She said to give it to her the next time I saw her or on the day of the event. Then, she texted me to tell me that she had made me her Woman Crush Wednesday. She sent me a screen cap of it but continued to say that she had to take it down after a bit to post a contest. She said that she hoped it helped me get more followers. I told her that I made her mine, too, and that I hoped she got some followers from me, even though I didn't have nearly as many followers as she did. At least she told me that she took it down and why. This made me feel a little better about the situation.

At that time, I was researching Splash Mountain-inspired outfits for the Club 33 event that I mentioned above, and the theme was "Critter Country." I found silly outfits that fit that theme online and began sending them to Crystal. She laughed and said, "Those are hilarious! We should go all out and dress up in costume that day and take tons of photos!" I agreed, and we planned to meet up in about a week or so to find the best Southern, "Critter-Country" style outfits. We were going to have the most fun we could have that day at Club 33.

The next day, Crystal texted me to set up a shopping spree for our Splash Mountain outfits. We planned to see *The Nightmare Before Christmas* at El Capitan before heading to Jet Rag to find our costumes. We met up at the Mansion on that planned morning, and I drove us to the theatre. While we were there, she asked me if I had been getting her movie night invitations again. I told her that since I was taken off of the list, I was only invited out to that one movie night to see *Labyrinth*. After having told me when I got kicked out that she had no power over the situation (which I knew from staff and girlfriends who used to live there that that was a lie), Crystal finally contradicted herself on the situation. She said, "This is stupid. I will talk to Joyce and make sure you get back on." Now, she didn't follow through with her claim right away, but I didn't expect her to. I thought it was pretty funny that she was contradicting herself back and forth so much about it. There was some odd reason floating in her head why she didn't want me there. Whatever the reason, I didn't care anymore. I was not stupid enough to pry, at all. In time, if she wanted, she would open the doors once again for me. If not, I didn't feel like I was missing out on anything anymore.

After sitting through the movie, which was awe-inspiring with special "4D" effects (wind, lightening, and light snow to accompany the movie), Crystal was completely insistent upon paying for everything. I tried hard to pay for, at least, the parking, but she wouldn't allow it. She also continued to pry and fish and ask me what I felt about every person in our lives, and I held my tongue as much as I could. For some reason, collecting my opinions on anyone and everyone seemed to be a hobby for her, and I tried desperately to answer her in an intelligent, yet honest way. Then she would always give me a neutral reply back (just a simple "they're okay" or "they're pretty nice") unless she despised that person, but it was rare she'd admit that she didn't like someone to me. (I'm sure this is because she knew how to protect herself, too.)

Next, we made our way to Jet Rag. We found the best "Critter Country" inspired outfits and had so much fun playing dress up. She told me that she loved the fact that we could just goof off together. My outfit wound up being a Southern-style, vintage, brown and white dress with a western, Winnie-the-Pooh vest over it. Crystal's costume was a purple prairie dress and a western-style vest to go over it. We both got bandanas and purses that looked like satchels. We were ready for Splash Mountain's Anniversary.

On November 12, 2014, I arrived at the Mansion at 10:30am to head out with Crystal. She was a little distressed because the dress she bought for the event was missing. She believed it had been brought to the dry cleaners by their staff, and she was in contact with them to make sure it came back in time. Well, it was now time to leave, and her dress was still missing. She put on a different dress and, the second she made it downstairs, they ran in with the appropriate dress. Talk about the last possible second. She gave a sign of relief, quickly changed, and we headed out to Disneyland.

The night before the event, Crystal had been on Instagram and saw a Disney account post a photo of the old Jack Skellington prop from the Haunted Mansion Holiday. It was, supposedly, hanging "for sale" in a cast-member store called Company D. Crystal panicked and tried to find a way in. She posted on her Instagram "If anyone can get me in Company D tomorrow, please let me know!" Of course, within seconds, she had requests flying in. The first person to reach out was already going there with his wife, and Crystal came up with a plan to meet him. So, the new plan of the day was to go to the Club 33 event and then head to Company D.

We made our way into the park on this beautiful day, and we went straight to the Club 33 door. They had us wait outside for quite a while before letting us in one party at a time. We thought that after all that waiting we'd be allowed to go right in and sit, but they still had us wait in the entrance hallway for thirty minutes before we were seated for lunch. We walked through the small reception room out into the Court of Angels where they had a cute "Splash Mountain" wooden backdrop set up for us to take a photo with. So, we did! Then, we headed up the stairs to be greeted with a stream of appetizers. There were stuffed mushrooms, beef tartar, crab cakes, and shrimp for us all to grab, and there was a very tasty apple lemonade to drink while we waited to be seated. Everyone was walking around and mingling. There was one waiter who worked at the new club who had a very sour, stuck-up face.

He came by with little, baby forks for us to use and offered one to Crystal. When she said, "No, thank you! I can just use my hands," he gave her the most disgusted look, which I couldn't tell if it was his normal, stingy face or if he was actually disgusted. He said, "Oh, okay…" in a flabbergasted tone as he strolled away from us. I couldn't help but chuckle at his astonished, fish-like expression as he walked away.

The new hallway into the dining room featured beautiful murals on the walls with peacocks and beagles painted on them. I pointed to the peacocks and said, "Aaaww," to which Crystal replied, "If I never see another peacock again, I will be grateful." You see, peacocks are all over the property of the Mansion, and their mating call sounds like someone screaming in pain.

There was a bluegrass band playing fun Disney songs, such as "Zip-a-Dee-Doo-Dah" and a country version of "Let's Go Fly a Kite" as we waited. They were blocking our way, keeping us out of the dining room until… they parted, and we all flew through into Le Grand Salon. Because space was limited for the event, they sat Crystal and me with another group of two. Our table companions were an awkward couple who, we soon found out, weren't actually a couple at all. There was, in fact, a lot of tension between the two of them. They couldn't stop telling us how much they were not dating as we ate our lunches.

For some reason, the appetizers had mixed very poorly within my stomach. In fact, I think the beef tartar was not good. I kept having to go to the bathroom throughout lunch, and my stomach was not happily greeting any of the food. There was all this nice, expensive food, and I was sad that my stomach wouldn't enjoy any of it.

They were supposed to be serving "Southern Cuisine," and I was excited because I grew up in the South. Instead, it was very stereotypical country-style Southern food. They started us with a crawfish bisque and some odd, mix-matched salad. Then, they gave us a choice of pheasant, venison, or sole. Since I could not see myself eating pheasant or venison (I am very sensitive to the meat that I eat—hence the getting sick off of the beef tartar), I ordered the sole. They had wines paired with each of the courses, but, on top of the fact that I don't really drink, my stomach was in no position to handle that.

Once the main course was complete, we went into Le Salon Nouveau (the new jazz club) to be given dessert and a presentation celebrating Splash Mountain. It was a pretty amazing show. Tony Baxter, the man who designed Splash Mountain, came in and spoke about the ride's design. He explained why they chose *Song of the South* and why the ride was laid out the way it is. It was very insightful. Plus, they showed us photos of the ride being made and pieces of *Song of the South* (which is a big deal because Disney will not sell this anymore due to it being racially insensitive). Disney approved a few scenes that were okay for us to see for the presentation. Then, at the end, Brer Rabbit came running out and bounced around. They announced that he would be downstairs for photo opportunities.

While we were in the presentation, one of the members sitting next to us started asking us if we were in the Club 33 member's-only Facebook group. We said that we were not, so he added us to the two "members only" groups. He added Crystal first and then turned to me. I told him that it was not necessary to add me (since I wasn't a member), but Crystal insisted and told me to do it. No one realized that I wasn't a member, so they began streaming my Facebook and Crystal's with messages and posts welcoming us into Club 33. I was now able to see the members-only information because of this incident.

As the presentation concluded, we headed down to the entrance of the Club to find Brer Rabbit. We took photos with him before heading out. It was at this point when Crystal needed to touch base with Eddie, the man she was talking to about going to Company D. We agreed to meet his wife and him in front of the Pirate's ride. We were near the entrance when they, immediately, recognized Crystal and flagged her down.

Now, the main risk of meeting with people who follow you on Instagram is that they could be big fans. Some fans are really great, while some cross a line. While Eddie and Sarah were very nice people, they were just that: big Crystal fans. We went on Big Thunder Mountain and Space Mountain with them before heading over to Company D. They were very nice and spent the afternoon pouring compliments on Crystal. While we were heading out, Sarah asked for a selfie with Crystal. Within seconds, she had posted it with the caption: "Me and my friend @crystalhefner at @disneyland #happiesplaceonearth #ridejunkies." Now, this was harmless and pretty sweet that she called Crystal her friend, and no one really cared about that.

Things got a little weird when we were driving to Company D, though. Crystal told them it was okay for them to hop in her car, and she would drop them off when we were done. From the back seat, Sarah took a photo of Crystal driving. She posted it with the caption: "Being driven around by @crystalhefner while listening to #Disney music. #heaven" Her friends commented, asking if they were actually legitimate friends. She replied, "Yes! I'm so excited."

We got to Company D, and it was great. It is a small warehouse for cast members only that has 50% off Disney merchandise that didn't sell well or that had been left over from the parks. There was also very affordable art there and a "caged area" with ride props and such. The Jack head was in the cage, and as much as Crystal wanted to buy it, it was not for sale. More than likely, it would be up for auction at the D23 fan club convention the following summer. Crystal spent a lot of money at Company D, and she got a cute little Snow White figurine for Sarah as a gift for what they had done for her. Sarah took this as a birthday present and posted it to Instagram as well, thanking Crystal for an amazing birthday present.

We made it back after an hour in Company D and dropped off Sarah and Eddie. To be kind, Crystal told Sarah that if she wanted a Club 33 reservation to just ask. She, immediately, came back with "Oh my gosh, yes! Next week for my birthday!" So Crystal set up the reservation that day with them in the car. She made their day. Then, as they were leaving, Sarah got a little too "fan girl" by telling Crystal how much they loved her and how she should invite them to a party at the Mansion. Crystal was very sweet and polite the whole time.

On the way back to the Mansion, we began discussing people again. As I said before, Crystal loved talking about people as much as she could. She would gauge how I felt about them before telling me how she felt about them. It was like she was always fishing with me. During this particular car ride, she explained to me that Hef grades girls on their appearance. You see, when you first come to the Mansion, Hef has a Polaroid taken of you. He puts a grade on your Polaroid. She said that one of the older FITS girls got a D twice, and she didn't know how she was still around. She began questioning, again, why they would take me off the list when there were so many girls who had been around for years. Despite the fact that I was onto her games, she kept questioning why they would do that to me and told me how silly it was. Then, she told me that Alicia was taken off the list at the same time that I was.

I went back into my head again. *Maybe Alicia wasn't the reason I was taken off of the list after all? Or maybe she was causing drama talking about me, so we were both removed? Maybe Crystal really was just testing me?* I was pretty sure, at this point, that I would never know the truth. Crystal even used this opportunity to tell me that Joyce might not like me. She said that Joyce could have cut me. (Which I know is not true, but I humored her.)

A few minutes later, she contradicted herself again about her ability to take people off the Mansion list. She told me that last year she was irritated with who was invited to Thanksgiving. So this year, she reviewed the list before people were invited and ran it by Hef to see if she could cut people, and she did. She complained that Joyce kept people on the lists who were favorites of hers and friends of hers, and Crystal got rid of several of them. Then she told me that she went into the office and demanded to review the Thursday night list, as it was her night. She said she demanded that I be invited, as I am her friend and it is her "girl's night" and her movies.

As we arrived at the Mansion and went inside, I had to change for an event I was going to that evening with Raquel. I found out that I had to leave immediately, as it was starting earlier than expected. It was bad timing because, if I didn't have to go, I was invited up to Crystal and Hef's room to help clean out her closet and vanity for a shoot for Life and Style Magazine that was taking place the following morning. It would have been fun to help clean and organize with my OCD. I was bummed I couldn't help.

In fact, Crystal told me that she emailed Hef our photos while we were at Disney. That evening, he walked into the closet where Crystal and her friend Paula were working, looked at the photos, and said, "Hey! That's not you!" pointing to Paula. Crystal laughed and told Hef that I had to leave.

Later that same evening, Crystal texted me, having seen the photo that Sarah posted of her driving. She asked me if it was cute or creepy. I told her it was cute, but, at the same time, her bragging that they were friends as if they were best friends, was a little much. She agreed. She was creeped out, but she still humored her by commenting on her photos. She refused to comment on the car photo, though, as she didn't even know that one was being taken.

The following night, as Crystal had promised, I was back at the Mansion to watch *Notting Hill*, which was playing at Crystal's Thursday movie night. It was funny, because it seemed that I was at the Mansion more now that I was kicked off the regular list than I ever was when I was on the list. I got there late, so I was at the smaller table rather than my normal place at the big table. Jeremy came with Veronica, who I was not fond of, and noticed that I was back. I'm pretty sure that Jeremy knew that I was taken off the list. He gave me a funny look, "Malorie, I haven't seen you up here for months..." I just replied that I had been too busy to come. I was not going to play his games if he was trying to play them. Veronica was being very nice. She kept trying to talk to me. I felt bad, but I was ignoring her to text as Crystal came down and texted me from across the room. She laughed because I was sitting with Joyce after the conversation we had had the day before. I told her that I came late, so that was the only seat left. I then told her that it was just my luck that Veronica would come with Jeremy and sit next to me. She was asking why Veronica was there on her night. I explained that Veronica was never on the list, she just came as Jeremy's date every so often so she could come up.

I was afraid that Crystal was going to keep Jeremy from bringing Veronica around after her reaction to her being there on one of her nights when she wasn't invited, so I tried to change the topic. Crystal finally snuck up from behind me, plopped on the chair next to me, and said to everyone there, "Haha! I'm texting Malorie from across the room. I might as well come sit with her." With that, we started talking. When we went in for the movie, she asked me to sit with her, again, as her mother was on the other couch. She had me sit between her and Amanda (her publicist) on the couch with Hef. At the end of the movie, she thanked me for coming. I thanked her for inviting me, and she said, "Malorie, I'm going to ask to have you back on all the nights. I think it's stupid they took you off." I told her it wasn't a big deal, but she insisted. I thanked her, knowing that she would never really ask.

It was around this time that I realized a sad truth. I was stuck in a never-ending cycle. Nothing changed at the Mansion; it was the same routine. Generally, I loved this, but not when I was being thrown around on and off the list in a painful circle. Part of me didn't want to go back on the list, as it was freeing only being obligated to come Thursdays. One day was enough. And, I'm sure I'd do something wrong and be thrown off again. It was a never-ending circle of movies, drama, and the same old routine, and I was stuck in it. Why did I stay? Why did I allow myself to put up with it? I knew that I would be thrown around in a circle over and over until that ultimate end was reached. It was only like this since I befriended Crystal. Before that, everything was wonderful. What had I gotten myself into?

I tried to reflect on myself and what I had been through. Perhaps I was staying around to please Crystal? That's what I did with Russell and Kristina; had I not learned my lesson? It was nice to see that I was still the same old person, but perhaps it was time I stood up for myself. Enough is enough, right? I needed to learn to cut ties with people when things got bad. True, I was still the same old girl from Virginia. I was happy that I hadn't changed. But, perhaps it was time to evolve a bit and stand up for myself?

# A Horrible Downfall

As I got closer to Crystal, I learned many things about her, which is to be expected whenever you get close to anyone. In her case, there were many things I learned that I did not like. For instance, no matter how often you hang out with her, she will never post photos with you. She was quick, however, to post people she had never met or barely knew as her "Woman Crush Wednesday" if they had as many or more followers than her. That way, she had a good chance they would post her back, and she would gain followers from them. So our endeavors together were never posted on any of her pages. She would, occasionally, share a Facebook photo I posted of the two of us, but of course that was only when she allowed me to be her friend on Facebook, which wasn't always the case. And, if she did share a photo, she would be quick to delete it a few days later. I felt like she wanted to hide our friendship all the time. But, in her defense, she did that to everyone, so I couldn't take it personally. She seemed to be obsessed with gaining followers no matter what that meant, and no one could get in the way of that.

In my opinion, Crystal also blamed everyone else for her mistakes and flaws. When she wanted things taken care of, she'd either have Joyce do it for her or she would blame Hef. For instance, she got upset that people who visited from time to time would take photos of Hef at random, as she was usually in them and not always looking her best. In response, she had Joyce send out a message to everyone that attended the mansion, saying that you could only take photos of people if they knew the photo was being taken and were okay with it. It was very clear what that message was about. There was another instance, later on, where she blamed Hef for something that I didn't believe was Hef. I believed she was covering up for her own feelings. I will describe that later in the chapter.

As December approached, Crystal contacted me one week wanting to go to a special event at the Disney Imagineer Studios. There was a special store for Imagineers that was opening to D23 fan club members one morning very early, and she wanted to get in on it. We got there when the event began, thinking we would be safe. Boy, were we wrong! We were numbers 543 and 544! There were 500 plus people in front of us, and they were letting 40 people in the store at a time. We were screwed. As we attempted to wait, we wandered the little peace garden they had there, and that was nice. Then, we saw that there was a Starbucks. The line was unbelievably long, but there was nothing else for us to do because we were waiting to get in the store, so we went in the Starbucks line. After having been in the Starbucks line for well over an hour (while discussing our dental surgeries, as Crystal was getting her Wisdom teeth out in a couple of weeks and had a lot of questions about it), someone pulled the fire alarm. We were forced to leave the building and our place in line. We were livid. We waited an hour and a half to get almost there only to be kicked out of our place at the front. With that, we gave up and left the event.

Now, around this time, Crystal and I had planned on doing the Disneyland Holiday Tour a couple of weeks later with Raquel, but, like anything she ever agreed to do with Raquel and me together, she bailed out. She had told me a few days before we went to this Imagineer event that she couldn't go, and the reason was because her sister was sick. Well, at least she gave me three weeks' notice so we could ask someone else. Raquel's husband joined us, instead.

Crystal's reason for not attending the tour didn't make any sense to me. She cancelled on me slightly before this Imagineer Store trip. We went to this Imagineer Store event on December 6th. We then went to Disney with the rest of her family on December 7th, but she cancelled our December 17th trip because of her sister's surgery, which took place around the 3rd or 4th of December. It was illogical, and I think the real reason was because of her social anxiety. I think that the thought of being around Raquel and me together, scared her. We were supposed to go to Club 33 with Raquel that day, so I shot Crystal a text when I went to work after our Imagineer Store adventure. I asked her if it was okay if Raquel and I still went to the club the day of the tour. Immediately, Crystal started waffling.

"I have to check how many reservations I have left. Since people were selling them and stuff, it's limited now, but I don't know how many it's limited to." She fumbled lies to me, as I knew this wasn't a true fact.

"Okay. Don't worry about it if it's a hassle or anything." I really didn't want to make an issue over this. It honestly didn't matter to me.

A few minutes later, she texted me again, "Sorry. I can't. Hef wants me to just have my guests go when I am there since I have had lots of problems with it."

"No worries."

"We can go any time when we are there together."

"Okay!"

Then, she went on a very long explanation, telling me a story about how Caya had a card on her account (which I knew was true) and abused her privileges. She claimed that, with that incident, Hef became in heavy control of her account. She said that she thought it cleared up so she let Eddie (the guy that got us into Company D) go, and it became an issue again, because they called to confirm. She said that Hef told her if we were really her friends we would wait to go with her.

Now, here's the deal: I know the first part was a lie for the following reason: as I mentioned before, I was added as part of the private Club 33 Facebook page. Crystal had encouraged me to be added, as I mentioned before, so I was. They posted harmless things there, so she didn't care; however, one of the members posted the new rules in the page. You see, Club 33 changed all of their rules and regulations in the beginning of 2015, pretty much cutting a lot of member privileges. They took away member cards, took away benefits, and more. Next thing I know, I hear that Crystal did not want me to know this, so she saw that this was posted and immediately "reported me" to the group as not being a real Club 33 member…so they dropped me. She stabbed me in the back to have the control she wanted. The only reason why I was upset was because she was the one who encouraged me to join that group. She acted like nothing happened, and I never confronted her about it because it wasn't my place to be a member of that group, anyway.

She neglected to delete me from a second Club 33-member group, however, which posted the same information for me to see. So I knew the new club rules, and I knew that they were not limiting reservations at that time. It was a lie. I'm not sure if she was going to use that lie and then go into the real reason, or if she just wanted an army of reasons why she couldn't let me go.

Regardless, as I mentioned above, it seemed that Crystal continually blamed everyone else for her problems. She had offered me the chance to go to the Club numerous times whenever I wanted, and I never took her up on it. The one time I had tried (because we were supposed to go with her and she cancelled), she used every excuse to keep her from looking bad by saying "No." I think the real reason she said "No" was because she wanted control over me. But, she was sure to blame Hef and Caya so that she came out the victim. It's never her decision—it's always Hef. Hef doesn't want her to do this. Hef doesn't want her to say that. I was over it. I just wanted real honesty. She texted me on and on about why it wasn't her fault and that she felt so bad. She wanted me to be sure to know that she was the victim. It really didn't matter to me, I just wished for honesty. I wasn't mad, but I felt that she was harboring resentment towards me because I had made her feel guilty by forcing her to say "No." I didn't see things ending well after that.

The next morning, we were all meeting at the Mansion at 6am to do the Disney trip with her family that I had discussed before. Facing her after the conversation we had and the Club 33 group drama was surprisingly easy. So much drama had happened in one day, but the Disney trip the following day seemed to make it better. The group for this trip consisted of her mother, her step dad (who is the sweetest man in the world), her nephew (who is our age), her publicist, Hef's secretary, Paola, and me. We got there in the magic morning hour to ride everything we could at California Adventure before the crowds came in. Then, we did a few rides at Disneyland before swinging by Club 33 to pick up merchandise. (At this point, I had become a frequent with Crystal at the club.) I got an amazing collectable Mickey Mouse stuffed animal with the 33 logo on his foot. I was really excited about that Mickey.

Then it was time for the reason we came that day: The D23 Ginger Bread House Event. We all met in a restaurant where they supplied us with jingle bells and chef hats. We spent a couple of hours eating lunch and enjoying building our own gingerbread houses. I had never made a gingerbread house like that before, and it was fun. We were afraid there wouldn't be enough candy, so we brought some of our own. Crystal had asked the butlers to pick some up for us the day before. They must have thought it would be funny to mess with us, so they bought candy sea turtles, sharks, and sea creatures. So... all of our gingerbread houses had lakes with sharks and sunbathing turtles.

That day was the first occasion in which I spent any real time with both Amandas (her publicist and Hef's secretary), and they were very sweet. We had a lot of fun together. Like always, Paola was fun, too, and Crystal's nephew was funny. As I said above, Crystal's stepfather is the nicest man in the world. He is so soft spoken, and he has a slight stutter. I will never forget when we took him to the Lego store at Downtown Disney. He was fascinated by all of the toys. He wandered around, purchasing multiple Lego sets, and showed them all to us with excitement.

We left the gingerbread house endeavors that day to see the Aladdin show. I had never seen the Aladdin show there, and it was excellent! After the show, we all went back to the Mansion. Crystal invited us to stay for the Sunday movie that night, but I had too much to do to stay.

After that trip, I was gone for two weeks in Virginia so I didn't see Crystal for about a month. We texted a bit, but that was it. In January, I went for a movie night, and she invited me to Disney with her the following week. I was so excited until she texted me the day before the trip to tell me that there was an issue with the guide. Because of this, we weren't going. My initial thought, because I was done trusting Crystal after the Club 33 group (and many other moments), was that she was betraying me again. I thought that she found someone better to bring, so she cancelled on me to bring them. That's how little I trusted her at that point. Come to find out, she was telling the truth. Shortly after, she texted me to invite me to go snowboarding with Caya, Melissa, and her. I had never gone snowboarding before, but I was happy to try any sport once. (That was the tomboy still in me somewhere.) With that, my doubt went away, and I accepted Crystal's invitation. Why I continued to go on with a relationship without trust is beyond me.

I arrived at the gates of the Mansion at 5am that following morning. Being just Crystal, Caya, Melissa, and I, I realized that she had invited me out with her intimate group. Was I becoming a part of it? Surely this was a test. I knew Caya relatively well from working with her at Bench Warmer, but I had never gotten to know Melissa at all.

While we waited to leave the Mansion, Charlie began freaking out. Charlie was following Crystal and barking like crazy. She was put off by his barking and kept yelling at him to stop. Her other puppy, Lady, kept dropping her ball by Crystal's feet. She explained to me that Charlie always knew when she was leaving, and it made him anxious. Because of this, he would follow her everywhere, barking, as if to protest her leaving. And, in Lady's case, she just always wanted attention. As we ate our breakfast and prepared to leave, I sat on the floor with Charlie and pet him. His barking subsided as my petting got more and more frequent. Then, Lady began dropping her ball at my feet, so I began throwing her ball to her every few seconds. Everyone else was blocking out the cries of the animals, but I wasn't used to it, and I didn't have it in my heart to ignore them when they wanted love.

As the sun began to rise, we left the Playboy Mansion and headed out to Big Bear. I anticipated that we would be snowboarding, as that is all Crystal spoke about before the trip; however, she told me she wanted to learn to ski and asked if I would ski with her. Skiing was something that I was familiar with, so I agreed. We listened to Disney music and had small conversations the whole way up. By the time we got up there, I was super carsick, so I was ready to get on solid land.

Once we checked in, we went to get our rental equipment. Without hesitation, Crystal led us up the ski lift to the top of the hill. I was under the impression that we were going to the bunny slope, as I told everyone that I hadn't skied in years, and Crystal had never skied before. Little did I know, they took us up to one of the bigger hills. Once we got up to the top, before we went down, they all decided that we were going to eat at a little cafeteria that we found in front of us. Unfortunately, food was not being served yet, so we had to wait. As we were waiting, we all migrated to a round table in the corner of the room. The chatter that we had been having turned into a pretty wild conversation.

Melissa asked me about Bench Warmer, and Crystal immediately turned to me and added, "Why doesn't Brian make cards of me anymore? Does he not want to pay me?"

I was a little startled, "You know... He is making more cards of you. He talked to me about it recently."

"Okay."

She turned away. Then, over the course of us waiting for our food (and I honestly don't remember how), the conversation took a very drastic turn.

Melissa and Crystal began talking about all of the drugs that they used to take when they were younger. Both of them admitted that they hadn't done any in years, but they began telling me about the experiences that they had while on drugs. Caya didn't contribute to the conversation (and, of course, I didn't either), but she kept the conversation rolling by asking questions about what it was like. They asked me if I had ever done anything.

I laughed and explained that I have never done drugs. I've never even smoked. They were even more surprised when I told them that I had never been drunk before either. Once the conversation ended, we packed up our things and ran to the slopes.

We found out that Crystal could not ski. Caya and Melissa left us in their dust as I was getting into the hang of being on skis again. Crystal couldn't get three feet without falling on her butt. We got to a steep, steep drop and found Caya and Melissa waiting for us. I took one look at the fall and told Crystal that we were never going to be able to make it down that hill alive at our experience level. She looked at me, "Are you sure? ... Yeah, I see your point! Let's get rescued!"

Earlier, on our way up the lift, we had an employee named Ryan go up with us. Crystal was excited because she, clearly, thought he was cute. I was not impressed. She was excited to call him to our rescue. Caya and Melissa went down the hill to get his assistance, and the two of us waited in the snow to be rescued.

As Crystal finished up with a random phone call, Ryan appeared. Ryan skied over and told us that they could not rescue anyone that wasn't a child on the snow mobile. So, he told us to carry our skis and cut through an area of the woods that would take us to an easier hill.

Once on the smaller hill, I had a much easier time skiing; however, I had to keep stopping so I didn't get too far ahead of Crystal, who was still falling. Finally, having given up on the skis, she took them off and walked down the hill with them. I skied alongside her. Part of the way down, again, Ryan found us and laughed, "You are still having trouble?" She explained that she could snowboard but that she had never skied. He walked us to the ski lift to send us back down on the "ride of shame" to the bottom of the hill. Crystal made it a game to wave at all the people we passed that were coming up on the ski lift as we were going down.

With that, we switched to snowboards. Crystal was, legitimately, good with a snowboard. I, however, was not. On my last trip down the mountain, I learned that I could only snowboard backwards. I was not capable of staying balanced with my weight on my heels, but, with my weight on my toes going down backwards, I found I could stay up the whole way down. It was very strange.

That night, on the way back, I fell asleep. Getting up early was not an easy thing for me, and snowboarding was a lot of work. That being said, I didn't talk much with the girls on the way home.

After this trip, out of nowhere, my relationship with Crystal dwindled. No surprise there, I guess. Like everyone else in her life, I came and went after a short visit. Our friendship just slowly died, and it was almost an abrupt ending just the same. I was a little upset because, for some reason, I really did like spending time with Crystal. She could be a lot of fun in person, but I was more relieved to get away than anything. At least I knew the games were over as I stopped getting invited to Crystal's movie nights, once again. You see, being engaged in a relationship with Crystal felt, to me, like a complicated relationship.

The good times were always really good, and the bad times were really bad.

# The True Ending

At the moment when I was sure that I would never see Crystal again, she did what she always did and surprised me. We were supposed to go to a Disney expo together on Sunday February 15th. I assumed that she was going to cancel on me, as that was the way our relationship had been going. I was going to ignore our plans and see if she would say anything. I anticipated her ignoring me; however, she texted me at 7pm the night before asking me what time I was going to get there. When I told her I didn't know yet, she asked who else I was bringing. I let her know that, as we had planned, it was just going to be me. At that moment she immediately decided that we should just meet there and hang out together at 9am, because she was getting in early because her friend was a vendor.

The following morning, we met up at 9am at the expo hotel and looked around. There were a lot of beautiful Disney art and collectibles there. She spent about $2,000 on Disney art, Small World Collectible dolls, and a lounge chair with Mickey ears all over it. I got a beautiful Cinderella motion ornament, an old *101 Dalmatians* Little Golden Book that I used to have, and an awesome metal sign that came from the Disneyland Resort. (Crystal's friend gets actual signs and merchandise from the park. He gave me an amazing deal on this parking sign which said, "Reserved for_____ Our Cast Member of the Year." I was going to paint my name in the name spot and put it in my garage, above where my car goes.)

When we were texting the night before, Crystal told me that she could only be there for an hour or so, and then she had to meet her friend. So I was anticipating leaving early to go back home and nap or to visit my husband, who was on set at this time. Little did I know, once she was with me, she changed her mind. She asked me if I was doing anything and then invited me to go with her to Disneyland after to meet up with her friend with her. I had no real plans all day, so, of course, I decided to go with her. We tried to get lunch reservations at both Ariel's Grotto and the Blue Bayou, but they were unable to get us any reservations on such a short notice. Because of this, we went and had lunch in the Salon Nouveau (the new lounge) at Club 33.

We arrived, waited in the Court of Angels, and had some delicious apple cinnamon drink before they came and took us upstairs into the lounge. We took a booth and each had a soup and salad. She began asking my advice as we ate. She told me that she had a friend who was gay. She knew that he was gay with her other friend, and that friend admitted it to her. But this friend wouldn't admit that he was gay to Crystal. She asked my thoughts. I told her that a friend is someone who you should be honest with. If he is really her friend, he should be open with her, especially knowing that she wouldn't judge him for it. I told her to just tell him that she knew and that she accepted him the way he was. She seemed quiet and reserved as we ate, but she seemed to happily accept my advice.

As we made our way out of the club, we stopped in the restroom, and Crystal met a fan in there. She stopped her and said, "Hi! I'm sorry...I'm obsessed with you!" With that, she gave Crystal a big, awkward hug. We could hear her in the hallway after she left the restroom telling her boyfriend about Crystal being in the bathroom. When we came out to leave, she asked for a photo. It was cute. I had never seen anyone get so excited about Crystal before.

After lunch, we met up with her friend and the friend's family, rode a few rides, and then headed out. As we were leaving, she wanted to stop for a chai, so we went into the Starbucks at Downtown Disney.

As we stood in line at the Starbucks, Crystal gained the courage, I'm guessing, she had been searching for at lunch and began confronting me out of nowhere. I think she took my "friends should be honest with each other" advice that I had just given her and used it on me. Now, I knew that something was wrong because I had been taken off of her movie night list, yet again. Plus, I had a feeling that she didn't trust me much because of the way she had been acting, and this proved it; however, she used this opportunity not to attack me or corner me, but to discuss our friendship. Perhaps she did want to work on our friendship? It took me off guard, but, once the day was over, I felt a lot better about everything.

First, she turned to me and said, "I've wanted to ask you about something. Miriam freaked out on me on my Facebook the other day. She went off about how someone said something to her about me and how I didn't like her.... And I haven't ever talked about Miriam to anyone except to you."

My honest truth on this matter is that I do not talk to Miriam about anything personal. I work with her, but I would never have said anything to her, so I assured Crystal that it wasn't me. She understood and seemed to be okay with my answer.

Then, she told me that there was one more thing she had been holding back for a long time. She told me that, a while after her birthday, two girls came to her and told her that I was saying that she was a flake because she didn't follow through with our plans. Apparently, because she was told this, she had texted me to explain the situation. So THAT was why she texted me that one night to explain. (I planned to go back and review those texts again once I made it home.)

I told her that I would never say anything behind her back that I wasn't willing to say to her face. Yes, I was a little upset about that incident, but if anyone heard me talk about it, it would have been me explaining the situation to Pam or Raquel, privately, at a Bench Warmer signing. If anyone else overheard, they were listening in on my private conversation, and they were making drama out of me being honest about my feelings with my friends. I told her it was not of any ill intent, and I was very sorry if it caused her stress.

Crystal replied by saying that she knows she's a flake, and it wasn't a big deal; she just wanted to hear my side.

Then, she continued to say the other reason she was cautious with me, aside from hearing these things, was because of Anna. Anna Sophia Berglund had shot for three of my projects this year, and Crystal could not stand her after their falling out. It really bothered her that I was around Anna, and, supposedly, she was afraid that Anna would turn me against her.

I let her know that when Anna was around, she never came up. We were not just sitting around talking about her. I told her that the last couple of times I saw her, we never even talked. It was quick filming— all work— and then she left. Crystal said that she understood that since there weren't many Playmates who were also real actresses, she understood why I would use Anna, but if she didn't mean that much to me like I was saying, she'd feel better if Anna wasn't around.

That was a lot to take in.

When I got home, I sent this text to Crystal, summing up our heart to heart, "Thanks for telling me about the expo today. And for lunch! I love my sign! It was so much fun. And, again, I'm really sorry if that birthday thing caused any stress. I really appreciate and enjoy our friendship... It would have been me explaining to Raquel or Pam why we didn't go and never would have been with any ill intent. And I promise the Miriam thing is not me. If anything like that is ever bothering you, please tell me. And I really enjoy our time together and love that you love Disney like me! I will let you know what my schedule looks like this week and maybe we can do Disney again!"

She replied, "Sorry for the drama stuff, but I'm happy we talked about everything. Yeah the Miriam thing I wasn't worried about I just deleted everything associated with her so it wouldn't happen again. I'm glad we talked and that we were able to and that makes me happy. Bottom line is, I really care about you and value our friendship."

It wasn't until after I got home that I remembered something that happened in the club. Crystal was explaining to me why she changed her Facebook name and deleted most of her friends. She told me, "People that I am friends with, like you, I'm going to see anyway. So why do I need Facebook for that?" It wasn't until right at that moment that I realized that she must have been explaining why she deleted ME from her Facebook! She deleted me? Sure enough, I checked, and she changed her name and deleted me (and almost everyone else associated with Playboy) from her Facebook. She kept Caya, her family, Paola, and the Amandas. That was it from our friends. Well, I knew that she could be irrational, and I was numb to it at this point.

Despite Crystal saying she wanted to work on our friendship, I was not invited around her again. I used this opportunity to try and shut her out of my life, but she wouldn't let me for a while. When I did not talk to her for a month, she would text me and tell me how much she missed me. But, when we tried to schedule something, she would never show up. I realized that her confronting me, despite what she said, must have been a resolution for her rather than an attempt to save our friendship. By deleting me from her Facebook, she deleted me from her life, just as easily. I missed the times we had together, because we did have fun together, but I was happy that the stress, anxiety, and worry that she brought into my life was over. I gradually stopped replying to her texts, and she slowly stopped texting me. That was our true ending.

# Reflection

After I had a chance to reflect on the situation with Crystal, everything made sense to me. I gave her way too much benefit of the doubt, and I expected too much good from her. She told me, during our confrontation, that the day someone told her that I called her flakey was the day that she texted me and explained the events of her birthday. Looking back at those texts, I saw that that was the EXACT same day that I was kicked out of the Mansion the first time. There was no denying it anymore: that was what originally got me uninvited. It was clear now that that was no coincidence. Not to mention, Alicia and Caya both had told me later that it was their fault. They were the ones who had been talking about me to Crystal and putting ideas in her head. So my theories were mostly correct. Alicia said that I was only after a friendship with people who could further me, after she didn't understand me not wanting to go to the clubs with her. Caya was her best friend, so she supported her on this. Once I confided to my friends around Alicia at a signing that Crystal had cancelled our plans on her birthday, she was quick to get the message back to Crystal that I mentioned it and was hurt by it. And the rest was clear.

Crystal heard something that I, supposedly, said about her, and I was kicked out of the Mansion without explanation... that same day! She, simply, texted me her side as if it came out of nowhere, without making it clear what was going on. Then she pretended that she didn't know I was kicked out. She blamed my banishment on Joyce, saying that maybe Joyce didn't like me. She tried to hint that it might have had something to do with Alicia—which it was Alicia who told her. But, truthfully... No, it was her! It was always her. She could have come and talked to me about it if she was really my friend. She could have confronted me and gotten my side.

She must have second-guessed her choice to kick me out when she added me back on her Thursday nights for a while. She didn't confront me about her issues, even as we hung out on a weekly basis, until over six months after I was kicked out, and she never admitted fault in kicking me out. But how could she not have, knowing that? That is not a friend. As I told Crystal that day, friends are honest with each other. I was stuck in a never-ending whirlpool that kept pulling me under the water and thrashing me back on top. I was Crystal's friend for that year because it suited her. After stepping back, I saw that she treated me like a toy. She played countless games with me. For what purpose? Was she really that bored?

I was a little ashamed of myself for giving her the benefit of the doubt. How did I allow myself to be treated that way? Why was I blind to so much as it was happening? Why didn't I stand up for myself?

I do not hate Crystal; I just think she was immature. After everything I saw, I felt that she was a manipulator and nothing more. I would have respected her had she just been honest with me from the beginning. She mistreated Trisha, Anna, myself, and many more along the way. But I wish her nothing but happiness in her years to come at the Mansion. I wasn't going to let the betrayal from Crystal knock me down.

If anything, my endeavors with Crystal made me a stronger person. After being able to reflect and see what I had gone through with her, I was more aware in the future of the things happening around me. It wasn't that I stopped trusting people, but I was more on my guard, and I knew what to look for. I learned to stand up for myself the next time something like that came around. After years and years of dealing with these types of situations, I have finally learned to stand up for myself. That is a wonderful, liberating thing.

I greatly value the time I had at the Playboy Mansion, and appreciate it more than anything. I was so lucky for so long to get to experience the amazing things that I did. From my journey there, I gained insights, true friends, and a time of my life. My friendships with Marston, Pamela, and Raquel are still things to be treasured, and I appreciate everything that Hef did for me. I appreciate a lot of the good Crystal did for me, too, I just wish I wasn't so naive to believe some of her lies. I'm proud of myself for, eventually, not replying to Crystal's texts and freeing myself of that dead relationship. I was proud of myself for being true and honest when Crystal confronted me.

And, when I really think about it, this is what I learned: I learned to appreciate what you have. Not even the wealthiest or the most powerful people are always happy. We all have problems, and you will be happiest living your days without worrying about what others think of you. Cutting Russell from my life was a blessing. Cutting Crystal from my life wound up being a blessing in disguise. After cutting Crystal from my life, a huge stress was released from me. I didn't have to worry about what she would think of me all the time. I found my way out of the horrible whirlpool, and I came out a stronger person.

When I look back on my time at the Mansion, I realize that the Mansion is what you make of it. There are so many girls that come out hurt, angry, and ready to slander every aspect of it. I think it was an amazing experience in my life. It was a place of happiness for me, because that is what I allowed it to be. I came in with excitement and an open mind. I got so many contacts and good experiences out of it because that was how I saw my time there: as a blessing. In return, I was blessed! I was strong and confident in myself, so I didn't allow Crystal or anyone else to tear me down, no matter how hard they tried.

What I'm trying to say is that the Mansion is not Heaven or Hell. We need to stop treating it like that. It is what you make of it. It is your own state of mind, meaning how you feel while you are there and how you want to see it is what it will become. You are the master of your own journey, and it's up to you where the Mansion or where anywhere else you travel in your life takes you. Even though I may miss The Playboy Mansion from time to time, I am in a different part of my life now. I have another journey to take on, and I will take what I learned from the Mansion with me in all of my future experiences. And, now, I happily close this chapter of my life.

# Epilogue: Thank You, Hef!

I can't help but look back at my teenage years. I see myself with old friends, all of us in the same place. We all had the same goals to travel and do wonderful things with our lives. I watch these friends of mine living average lives, getting married, having children, and changing their dreams to fit their new ideals. That is absolutely fine and wonderful for them, but that just isn't for me.

How did we start at the same place and wind up with our dreams so far apart? Here I am, living day by day in Los Angeles. I am planning trips, doing autograph signings at Comic-con, and flying home on a whim for a few days to see everyone. My life has definitely been one big, unexpected adventure, and I don't ever want it to be any other way. I want every moment to be extraordinary! And, so far, it has been.

I feel that I have Playboy to thank for a lot of that. It's silly to some, but winding up where I was at the Mansion was definitely a dream of my teenage self. To have that come true is an inspiration to lead me forward on new roads of my life. Here I am living my life one adventure at a time. To me, personally, I would never live any other way. And, for that, I truly have to thank Hugh Hefner. To me, Hef was an inspiration. He was always very kind to me. He allowed me into his world and gave me many happy memories. Thank you, Hef, for everything. You truly are a great man.

# About the Author

Malorie Mackey is an actress and model based out of Los Angeles, California. Malorie grew up in Richmond, Virginia where she loved sports, the outdoors, animals, and all forms of art. She took to acting at a young age, so it was no surprise when she decided to go to college for theatre. While in college, Malorie studied body movement with the DAH Theatre in Belgrade, Serbia, voice in Herefordshire, England with Frankie Armstrong, and the business of theatre in Buenos Aires, Argentina. Malorie moved from the East Coast to Los Angeles after receiving her BFA in Theatre Performance from Virginia Commonwealth University. Upon arriving, Malorie participated in the Miss California USA 2011 Pageant where she won the "Friend's Choice" Award (popular vote) and received a beautiful award for it. Since being on the West Coast, Malorie can be seen working on many Indie films, such as the Sci Fi Movie "Dracano." Most recently, Malorie starred in the Biography Channel show "My Haunted House" and the TV Pilot "Model Citizen" with Angie Everhart. She ended this past year working on three Indie Films: "The Martini Shot," "The Taker," and "The Summerland Project." Throughout her experiences, Malorie has kept diligent journal entries. It was these entries that became "My Playboy Story: Hopping from Richmond to Hollywood."

Malorie is inspired to continue writing. Next on her docket is to create a travel journal and, from that, a video travel blog. Stay tuned as Malorie travels the World making this dream a reality.

Printed in Great Britain
by Amazon

44224174R00108